INTRODUCTIOI

Megawords introduces procedures for teaching the reading and spelling of multisyllabic words through a multisensory approach. The program is the result of our experience teaching learning disabled children and adults. However, the techniques described will be useful to teachers of any population for which the goal is word attack skills for words with more than one syllable.

In working with learning disabled students, adults, and others with reading and spelling difficulties, we noted a lack of appropriate materials for teaching the reading and spelling of multisyllabic words. Numerous programs exist for instruction of phonic generalizations found in one-syllable words. While many materials include phonic elements of multisyllabic word patterns, few provide a format to assess skills, pinpoint weaknesses, teach required subskills, and monitor progress systematically. The dearth of materials for teaching skills in this area is a major problem for teachers whose students have reached a fourth- or fifth-grade reading and/or spelling level. Many students have difficulty advancing beyond this level, at which mastery of multisyllabic words becomes necessary. Our need to create a program to teach the more advanced reading and spelling skills became paramount.

At first it seemed impossible to design a structured format for teaching multisyllabic words because of their phonic complexity. As we developed the program, however, it became clear that the English language could be analyzed into components that demonstrate an amazing degree of regularity and consistency. We developed controlled word lists that build sequentially on phonic and structural elements. Some words are appropriately placed on more than one list. Some lists include words with phonic elements that are not focused on until later in the sequence. Though the lists are not perfectly inclusive or exclusive, each emphasizes a significant and recurring phonic element of the English language. Students can be encouraged to add new words to lists as they study them.

GENERAL DESCRIPTION OF *MEGAWORDS*

Megawords combines several principles found to be effective in teaching students with language learning difficulties. These principles, combined and specifically applied to the teaching of multisyllabic words, make *Megawords* unique.

- *Megawords* teaches phonic regularities. The lists are structured according to phonic elements. This approach stresses the teaching of rules and generalizations as a tool for sounding out and spelling unfamiliar words. The words are not to be taught as sight words unless indicated.
- *Megawords* is multisensory. Specific teaching instructions are provided to ensure that students use their auditory, visual, and kinesthetic modalities when learning a skill. The process of seeing, saying, hearing, and writing is a major key to success. Thus, the students practice spelling the words as they learn to read them.
- *Megawords* is systematic. There is no guesswork as to what students need to be taught or when to advance them through the program. A skills Check Test assesses each student's skills by pinpointing deficits and identifying specific instructional goals. Systematic monitoring of progress by use of the Accuracy Checklist for recording accuracy and of the Proficiency Graph for recording reading rate is an integral part of the program.
- *Megawords* is task analytic. The words on each list are analyzed and broken down into their component subskills and presented in sequential learning steps. Though the final objective is for students to read and spell the words with automaticity, they often need specific instruction on the intervening steps. When they use this method, their success is guaranteed.

- *Megawords* is adaptable to the individual's needs. The task analytic nature of the program makes this possible. Some students may master a word list with minimal drill on the sequential learning steps. Others will require more instructional time on each step. Goals for accuracy and proficiency are determined on an individual basis.
- *Megawords* is adaptable to the teacher's needs. It may be used for classroom instruction or for one-to-one tutoring. In a classroom setting, students can chart and graph their own progress. They can also learn to time each other for proficiency and to test each other for accuracy. The charts and graphs allow easy monitoring of the progress recorded by the students. The word lists can serve as a supplement to the regular reading program and the sequence can be adapted to correspond to other materials.
- *Megawords* encourages student involvement. Most students are motivated to progress when goals are identified for them. The structured format of this program specifies what is to be learned and how well it is to be learned. Because students can monitor their own progress, they can move at their own pace rather than that of the class average. Group or individual rewards for mastering skills can be used to motivate students.
- *Megawords* may be used by paraprofessionals. Teacher's aides, volunteers, and peer tutors can easily follow the instructions. Explanations for administration of the Check Test, teaching concepts, and monitoring progress are written in clear and simple language. With a modicum of effort, teachers can supervise and train paraprofessionals to use *Megawords* so that instruction can be individualized.

OVERVIEW OF TEACHING STRATEGIES

Megawords teaches the reading, spelling, and contextual use of multisyllabic words through a systematic progression of skills. Each book focuses on a distinct group of phonic skills; teaching strategies throughout the program are uniform.

For multisensory teaching to be successful, students need to practice spelling words while they learn to read them. This procedure provides the necessary simultaneous input through all the processing channels (visual, auditory, and kinesthetic). However, the approach used to teach spelling to low-skilled students differs in emphasis from that used to teach them reading. For reading, the goal is to teach students word attack skills that they can apply to decoding (sounding out) unfamiliar words. Thus, it is desirable to present to the students a large number of words that they may never have seen before in order to challenge their understanding of the concepts taught.

In contrast, the number of words required for spelling mastery should be limited for low-skilled students because spelling is a much more complex skill. Multisyllabic words frequently contain the schwa sound, which can be spelled with any of the five vowels. While this does not typically present a reading problem for students, it is a major barrier for those students who must learn to spell phonetically. This difficulty also applies to other vowel and consonant sounds that can be spelled in more than one way. The spelling task is usually further complicated by students' not receiving immediate feedback on their performances. For these reasons it is not feasible for severely learning disabled or low-skilled students to learn the correct spelling of all the words on the lists. Rather, students should learn to spell a limited number of useful words *well*. On each list we identify with an asterisk *practical spelling words* that the students are likely to use in writing. Teachers and students should feel free to add to or delete these words to suit their needs.

The procedures for using the *Megawords* materials are outlined below. You should familiarize yourself with these teaching strategies before using the program.

ASSESSMENT OF READING AND SPELLING SKILLS

Each book contains a detailed Check Test, which will specifically pinpoint skill deficits and, thus, identify which lists should be the focal point of instruction. This Check Test should be given as a pretest before students start a book. It can be readministered after students complete the book if posttest scores are desired. The Book 7 Check Test and instructions for administration are found on pages 10-11.

LEARNING STEPS

A discussion of relevant rules and concepts introduces each list. Six sequential learning steps follow; they lead to the final objective — reading and spelling words with automaticity. This task breakdown analyzes words according to their phonetic elements and then presents them in a parts-to-whole fashion.

Worksheets for each learning step enable students to acquire the necessary skills gradually. In this way, they experience greater success. Some students may proceed through all the steps rapidly or may even bypass some steps. Others may require prolonged drill and supplemental activities. Pacing will depend on the individual student's needs.

The Task Breakdown for Teaching the Coding of Multisyllabic Words on page 4 summarizes the six learning steps that are the backbone of *Megawords*. Each step includes both a decoding (reading) and an encoding (spelling) task. The left half of the chart indicates the decoding subskills; the right half, the encoding subskills. The tasks required at each step are as follows:

STEP 1. Work with the Isolated Word Parts

Drill on the isolated word parts is a necessary first step. This may entail identifying types of syllables or working on prefixes, suffixes, or special vowel and consonant combinations. Worksheets require the students both to read and spell the word parts. In addition, we recommend that students get additional practice on the isolated parts by using drill cards. Instructions for using drill cards in teaching specific skills are provided in each book.

STEP 2. Work with the Combined Word Parts

For this step, students are required to recognize word parts within words, combine them, and read a whole word. The reverse procedure is required for spelling: the teacher dictates a whole word and the student must isolate and spell the word parts. At first, students should say the isolated word parts aloud before spelling them. Eventually, they can say them to themselves. Practice with common spelling patterns for the schwa sound is included when relevant. This step is crucial and should not be bypassed.

Students are sometimes asked to mark vowels in words with an unaccented syllable. Some dictionaries list both the schwa and the soft-*i* sounds as acceptable pronunciations and some vary on the choice. Regional accents also affect the pronunciation of these words. For these reasons, do not insist that students always know the technically correct vowel sound as long as they can decode the word.

In Step 2 — Reading, words are presented as detached syllables as an intermediate step to help students identify the correct vowel sound before having to tackle whole words. You may notice that syllabication in *Megawords* is closer to that used for hyphenation than that found in pronunciation guides in a dictionary (*chat-ter* rather than /chat•er/, *dis-cus-sion* rather than /dis•kəsh•ən/). Syllabication is presented as simply as possible to avoid confusing the student with technical syllabication rules.

STEP 3. Work with the Whole Word

If students have had sufficient drill on Steps 1 and 2, reading and spelling the whole word should be relatively easy. For reading, they practice applying relevant word attack skills. Worksheets require them to divide whole words into syllables and to pronounce them. The spelling worksheets for Step 3 focus on words frequently used in writing. Students practice spelling the recurring phonic elements in common words. Spelling rules and generalizations are also presented in Step 3. Proofreading, the detection and correction of spelling errors, is a necessary and important skill for all students. Step 3 exercises provide practice in this skill.

TASK BREAKDOWN FOR TEACHING THE CODING OF MULTISYLLABIC WORDS

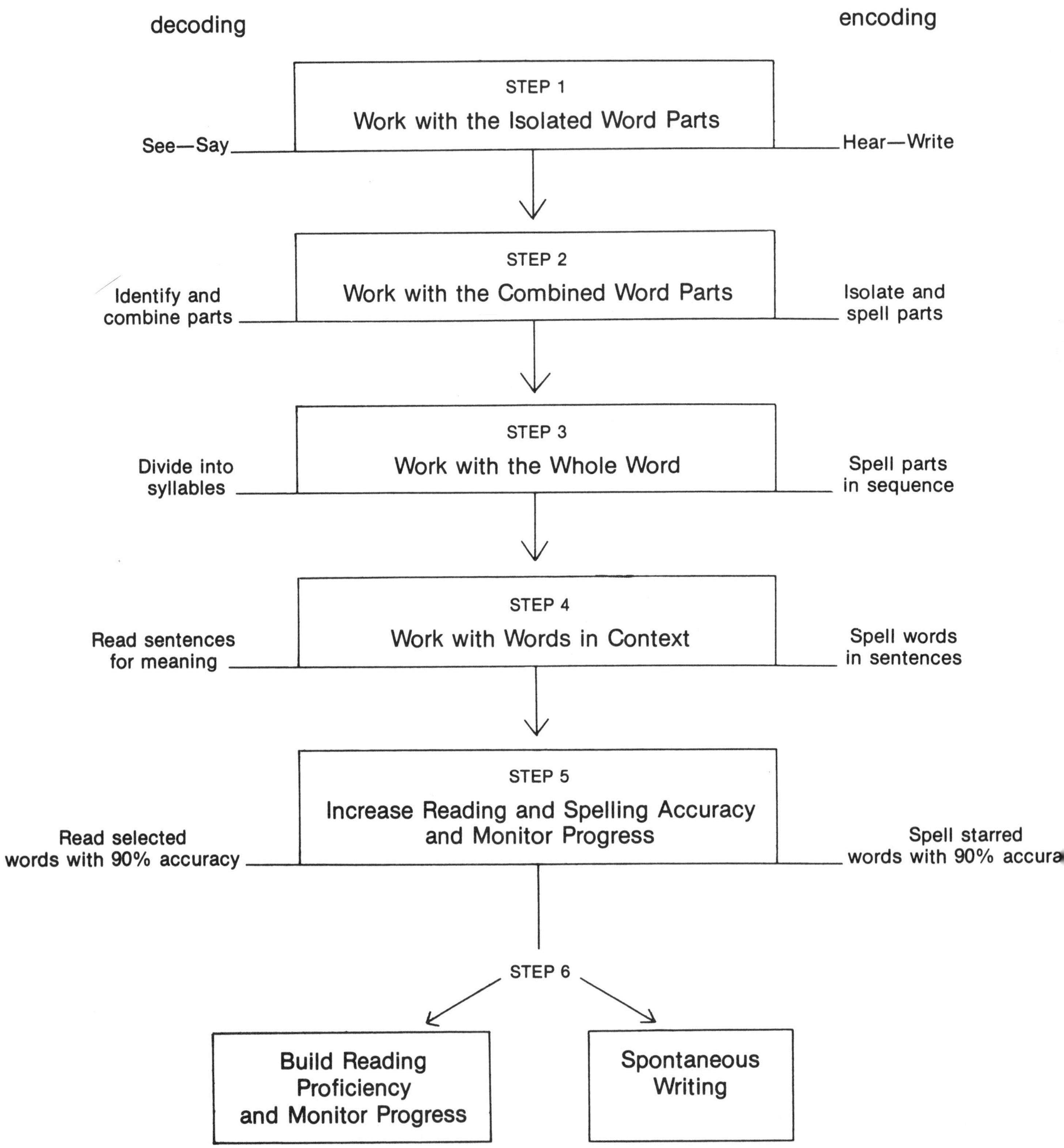

STEP 4. Work with Words in Context

This step provides an opportunity for students to apply their coding skills by using the words in context. Worksheets on vocabulary encourage them to learn word meanings from context as well as to develop dictionary skills. Reading and spelling sentences that emphasize the specific phonic element in each list are also part of this step.

STEP 5. Increase Reading and Spelling Accuracy and Monitor Progress

Students who have successfully completed Steps 1 through 4 are ready for a skill check on reading and spelling. Randomly select ten words from the list for the reading skill check. Ten starred words from the list can be dictated to test spelling accuracy. Skill checks should be repeated until students have achieved 90 percent accuracy or better.

The columns of many of the lists are organized according to vowel sound, prefix, or suffix. Some students may find it less frustrating to read *down* the columns initially, focusing on one pattern at a time. Subsequently, they can read the list by rows, alternating the word patterns.

Have your students record their progress in reading and spelling accuracy on the Accuracy Checklists. A copy of the Accuracy Checklist is provided on page 69 and in the student's workbook. Reading and spelling accuracy scores should be recorded to the right of the Check Test Scores column. These scores can be written as fractions: number correct over number attempted. The date when an accuracy check is done should be noted as well. When students have achieved 90 percent accuracy, they can shade in the box to indicate mastery. The sample Accuracy Checklist below demonstrates its use for record keeping.

The Accuracy Checklist is essential for monitoring your students' progress. It not only enables you to make appropriate instructional decisions but also provides valuable feedback to your students that they are, indeed, improving their skills.

ACCURACY CHECKLIST

Megawords 7, Lists 34–38

Student Sue Smith

Record accuracy score as a fraction: $\frac{\text{\# correct}}{\text{\# attempted}}$

List	Examples	Check Test Scores Date: 9/8		Reading			Spelling		
		Reading	Spelling	9/8			9/10	9/12	9/15
34. Unaccented *i* = /ə/ or *ĭ*	arbitrate quality political	5/5	3/5	mastered			7/10	8/10	10/10
35. Unaccented *i* = /ē/ and Unaccented *u*	zodiac continual	3/5	2/5	9/10 7/10	9/12 9/10		9/17 5/10	9/19 7/10	9/22 9/10

STEP 6. Build Reading Proficiency, Monitor Progress, and Encourage Spontaneous Writing

Research indicates that automaticity of decoding skills facilitates reading comprehension and is often a prerequisite to the more complex comprehension skills of reasoning and inference.[1] Students' skills must be automatic (proficient) before they can comprehend a passage or progress to more difficult skills. Thus, once students have demonstrated that they can read the word lists untimed with 90 percent accuracy, they should work on increasing their reading speed by doing frequent rate timings. In our experience, repeated practice and drill are more effective than direct instruction for building proficiency.

Use a stopwatch or second hand to time students as they read the list for a minute. A warm-up timing can be used for practice before doing a second, official, timing. If students finish the list in less than a minute, they should return to the beginning and continue to read until the time is up. Progress is then recorded on the Proficiency Graph, indicating the number of words read correctly in a minute as well as the number of errors. A goal of forty-five to fifty words per minute with two or fewer errors on two of three consecutive days is realistic for most students. This goal can certainly be adjusted for individuals. A sample Proficiency Graph is on page 7. A blank Proficiency Graph is on page 71 and at the back of the student's workbook.

Giving students sufficient practice in spelling words helps the spelling process become automatic. They are then able to concentrate on the content of what they want to express in writing. Their ultimate goal is being able to use correctly spelled words to convey their ideas. Although worksheets on written expression are not included in this program, you should encourage your students to spell the newly learned words in their written work. Creative writing assignments in which students try to include as many words as possible from a given list will provide such an opportunity.

ANALYSIS OF STUDENT PROGRESS FOR DECISION MAKING

Once students have attained 90 percent accuracy in reading words and are working to increase their reading proficiency, instruction should begin on the concepts of the next word list. This way, they will be learning new skills as they improve others. Typically, reading accuracy will be achieved prior to spelling accuracy. Thus, an individual might be working on spelling with List 2, on reading proficiency with List 3, and on reading accuracy with List 4. When you introduce new concepts, include the spelling tasks even if the students are still working to achieve spelling mastery on earlier lists.

If students are not achieving accuracy or proficiency goals, a teaching intervention is necessary. If a student's reading and/or spelling accuracy is not improving, more drill should be done on the learning steps. You can make up games and other creative activities to work on the necessary concepts. Error analysis can help pinpoint the areas of concern. For example, review of a student's mistakes in spelling might reveal difficulty in spelling a specific schwa ending pattern such as *-al* or *-on*. You can then provide the necessary drill to remedy the problem.

Lack of progress in reading proficiency also demands attention. If students are making more than four errors on timed readings, discontinue timing them and focus your instruction instead on reading accuracy. Identify and analyze the errors and concentrate your teaching on the specific problem areas. If errors are few but the students are not meeting projected goals, they probably need more practice with the words. Marked improvement can often be made if the students practice the word lists at home. Offering rewards, such as special classroom privileges, for attaining goals is also an effective technique. In some cases, it may be appropriate to lower proficiency goals for students who are having difficulty.

[1]E. Haughton, "Aims — Growing and Sharing," in Jordan et al., *Let's Try Doing Something Else Kind of Thing*, Arlington, Va.: The Council for Exceptional Children, 1972.
Barbara Bateman (ed.), *Learning Disorders*, Vol. IV, Seattle, Wash.: Special Child Publications, Inc., 1971.
S.J. Samuels and Patricia Dahl, *A Mastery Based Experimental Program for Teaching Poor Readers High Speed Word Recognition Skills* (Research Report #55), University of Minnesota, 1973.
C. Starlin, "Peers and Precision," *Teaching Exceptional Children*, Vol. 3, No. 3, pp. 129-140, 1971.

PROFICIENCY GRAPH

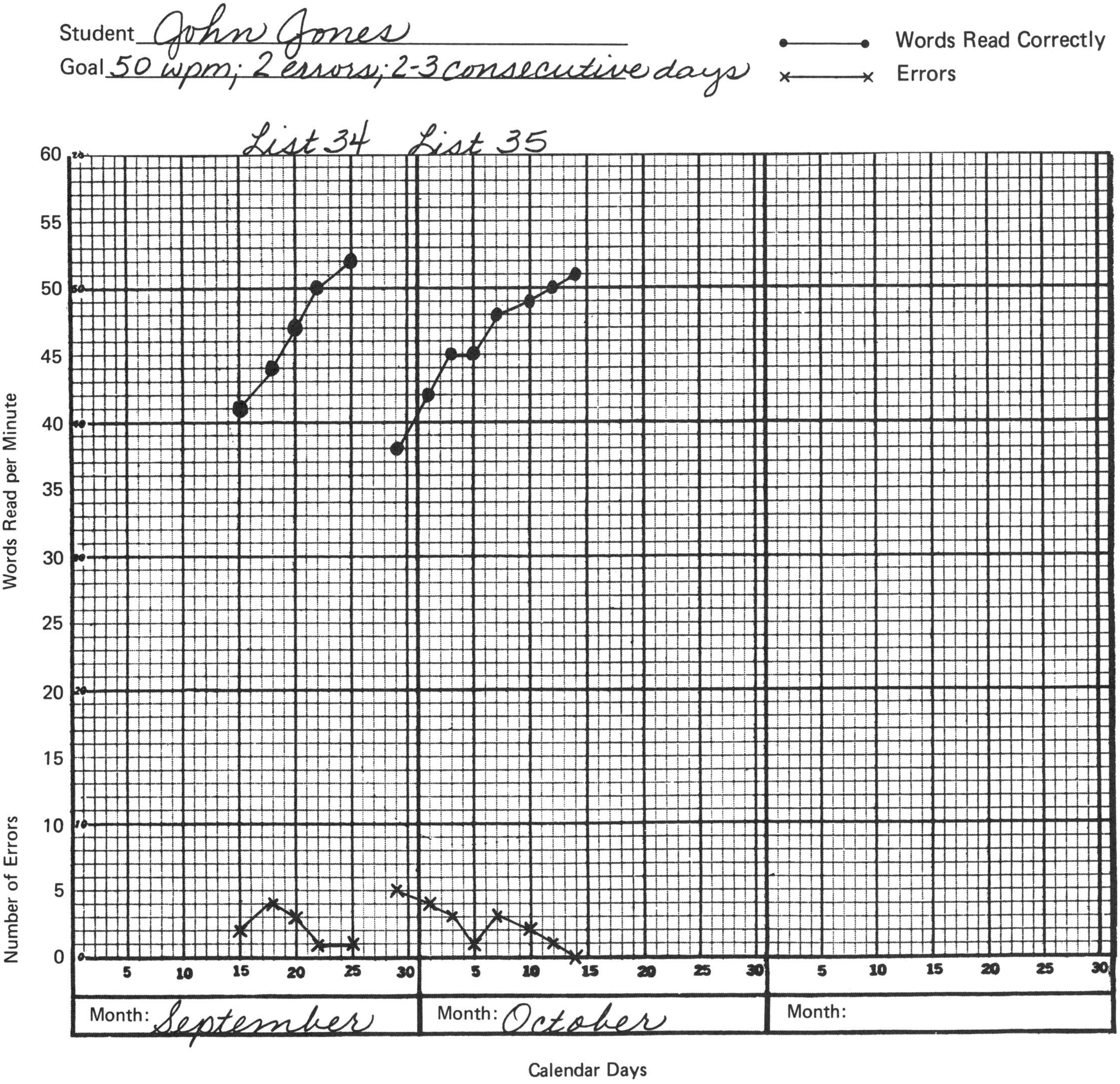

STUDENT INVOLVEMENT

Student involvement is a *must* throughout all of the learning steps just discussed. Students should be aware of their Check Test results, what they know, and what they need to learn. They should be aware of their progress in both reading and spelling accuracy and proficiency. They should know that the learning steps are divided into small parts to help them reach the ultimate goal of reading and writing fluently. We suggest that the teacher either read To the Student at the beginning of the student's workbook with the students or paraphrase and discuss it.

SPECIAL CONSIDERATIONS FOR *MEGAWORDS 7*

Megawords 7 (Lists 34–38) focuses on unaccented *i* and *u* and on advanced words with the vowel/vowel (V/V) syllabication pattern. Much of *Megawords 7* is devoted to various sounds of unaccented *i. Megawords 7* is, in many ways, a logical extension of *Megawords 3* with more advanced unaccented endings and unaccented middle syllables.

Unaccented *i* as /ə/ *(animal)*, as /ē/ *(studio)*, and as /y/ *(million)* are discussed. Common endings such as *-ity (reality)*, *-ical (political)*, *-iate (immediate)*, and *-ious (furious)* are practiced to reinforce spelling skills. Since *i* can be pronounced several ways, students need to be flexible in decoding these words: "If one way doesn't work, try another." Students learn the most likely spelling of certain sounds by learning common patterns.

Unaccented *u* in words such as *manual* and *popular* is also discussed. More complex V/V words such as *dialect* and *cooperate* allow review of concepts first learned in *Megawords 1*, List 8.

Some of the endings and middle syllables in *Megawords 7* are not spelled the way they sound or pronounced the way they look. Students who have a rudimentary knowledge of phonics but who are unaware of the more complex patterns tend to misspell and mispronounce these words (p-a-s-h-u-n-t for *patient*, s-t-a-d-e-u-m for *stadium*, o-p-i-n-y-u-n for *opinion*). However, once they learn the patterns, they are suddenly able to read and spell whole new groups of words with ease.

Games and charts are excellent reinforcement activities for *Megawords 7*. Adaptations of Crazy Eight, Go Fish, or Old Maid work well and are enjoyable. Cards with the same ending or unaccented vowel can be considered the same suit. Games such as Jeopardy can be adapted so that students can choose to read a $50 word such as *coagulation* or a $5 word such as *casual*. Students often enjoy making wall charts with a large number of words with a specific ending. Students also enjoy reciting long lists of semi-rhyming words that follow a pattern and are proud when they demonstrate mastery of the word list in either reading or spelling.

The unaccented vowels in *Megawords 7* are often "connectives," single vowels that come between the root and suffix of Latin and Greek words. In effect, they connect the root to the suffix and make the word easier to pronounce. The concept of connectives or, more loosely, "vowel connectors" helps show students how these vowels join word parts to make them easier to pronounce. Words like memorial, superstitious, and brilliant are examples with true connectives. Technically, however, many *Megawords 7* words do not fit the definition of *connective*, "joining a known vowel to a known ending," yet *do* contain the unaccented vowel with the noted vowel sound. *Piano* contains an *i* as /ē/, which precedes a syllable beginning with a vowel (List 35) but, of course, no root *p* or suffix *ano* exits. Therefore, we reluctantly gave up the label "connective" for these lists and decided upon the more cumbersome yet more etymologically accurate term "unaccented vowel." However, if the term "connective" or "vowel connector" helps your students better understand the common features in Lists 35, 36, and 37, feel free to use it.

SUMMARY OF ACCENT PATTERNS

Accented Syllable—An accented syllable is pronounced as if it were a one-syllable word with a clear vowel sound according to its syllabic type *(ac´ tive, com plete´, ser´ vant, loy´ al)*.

Unaccented Syllable—An unaccented syllable is pronounced with a schwa /ə/ or short-*i* /ĭ/ vowel sound regardless of its syllabic type *(rib´ bon, op´ po site, in de pen´ dent)*.

Accent Patterns—The dark lines and accent marks in this book are accent patterns (__´ __). Each line stands for one syllable. The accent mark shows which syllable is accented. Learning to place the accent on the proper syllable will help you recognize most multisyllabic words. The accent patterns below will help you determine which syllable in a word is accented.

Primary Accent—A strong stress on a syllable in a multisyllabic word.

Secondary Accent—A weaker stress on a syllable in a multisyllabic word.

General Guideline—In two- and three-syllable words, accent the first syllable. Then pronounce the first vowel as if it were a short, long, *r*-controlled, or double-vowel sound in a one-syllable word. If that doesn't make a recognizable word, accent the second syllable, and pronounce the second vowel according to its syllabic type.

Accent Patterns for Two-Syllable Words

1. Accent on the first syllable (—´ —)
   The accent is usually on the first syllable in two-syllable words *(stan´ dard, sis´ ter, dol´ lar).*

2. Accent on the second syllable (— —´)
   Two-syllable words that have a prefix in the first syllable and a root in the second syllable are usually accented on the second syllable *(ex tend´, con fuse´).*

3. Accent on either the first or second syllable (—´ — or — —´)
   If a word can function as both noun and verb, the noun is accented on the prefix *(con´ duct)* and the verb is accented on the root *(con duct´).*

Accent Patterns for Three-Syllable Words

1. Accent on the first syllable (—´ — —)
   The accent is usually on the first syllable in three-syllable words. The unaccented middle syllable has a schwa sound *(vis´ i tor, char´ ac ter).*

2. Accent on the second syllable (— —´ —)
   The accent is usually on the second syllable (the root) in words that contain a prefix, root, and suffix *(de stroy´ er, in ven´ tor).*

Accent Patterns for Four-Syllable Words (— —´ — —)

1. The accent is usually on the second syllable in four-syllable words *(in tel´ li gence, sig nif´ i cant).*

Special Accent Patterns for Words of Three or More Syllables

Accent patterns for words longer than two syllables are often governed by a specific ending pattern or an unaccented vowel.

1. Accent with the ending *-ic*
   Accent the syllable just before the ending *-ic (fran´ tic, e las´ tic, en er get´ ic, char ac ter is´ tic).*

2. Accent with the ending *-ate* /āt/
   In three-syllable words, the first syllable has a primary accent and *-ate* has a secondary accent *(vi´ o late´).*
   In four-syllable words, the second syllable has a primary accent and *-ate* has a secondary accent *(con grat´ u late´).*

3. Accent with schwa endings
   Schwa endings (and schwa syllables) are never accented. The accent falls on another syllable in the word *(pleas´ ant, in´ no cent, ex ter´ nal, ap pren´ tice).*

4. Accent with the endings *-tion, -sion, -cian*
   Accent the syllable just before the endings *-tion, -sion,* and *-cian (pol lu´ tion, im pres´ sion, ad min is tra´ tion, e lec tri´ cian).*

5. Accent with the ending *-ity* /ĭ tē/.
Accent the syllable just before the ending *-ity* (*qual´ i ty, ac tiv´i ty, per son al´ i ty*).

6. Accent in words with an unaccented middle syllable
Accent the syllable just before the unaccented middle syllable with *i* as /ə/, *i* as /ē/, and *u* as /ə/ or /ū/ (*sim´ i lar, aud´ i ence, par tic´ u lar*).

7. Accent in words with *i* as /y/
Accent the syllable just before the unaccented syllable with *i* as /y/ (*com pan´ ion, in con ven´ ient, mem or a bil´ ia*).

8. Accent in words with *ti* or *ci* as /sh/
Accent the syllable just before a final syllable with *ti* or *ci* as /sh/ (*fi nan´ cial, pres i den´ tial*).

CHECK TEST: LISTS 34–38

ADMINISTERING THE CHECK TEST

The Check Test informally assesses a student's ability to read and spell words that follow the patterns presented in *Megawords 7*. Although the reading test must be administered individually, the spelling test can be administered to a group.

To test reading, give the student the Student's Reading Copy[1] and instruct him or her to read down the columns. Use the Examiner's Recording Form[2] to note errors and mark the number correct. Enough space is provided after each word to write the student's responses so that errors can be analyzed later.

To test spelling, give the students blank paper and tell them to number from one to five, five times. Dictate the following words to assess their ability to spell frequently used words that follow the patterns presented in *Megawords 7*.

34. Unaccented *i* = /ə/
1. substitute
2. activity
3. necessary
4. participate
5. majority

35. Unaccented *i* = /ē/ and *u*
1. serious
2. immediate
3. usual
4. popular
5. inferior

36. Unaccented *i* = /y/
1. convenient
2. opinion
3. senior
4. brilliant
5. William

37. *ti* and *ci* Endings
1. delicious
2. patience
3. especially
4. residential
5. ambitious

38. Advanced V/V Combinations
1. theater
2. realize
3. science
4. cooperate
5. ideal

Share the test results with your students so that they become aware of the specific word patterns that they need to learn or review. Be sure constantly to reassess the students' skills as you work with them. Often you will discover strengths or weaknesses that were not revealed in the Check Test results.

[1]The Student's Reading Copy is on page 75. It may be removed and inserted in a plastic cover.

[2]An Examiner's Recording Form appears on page 73 and at the end of each student's workbook. Remove the student's form for the Check Test and keep it for your files. One side can be used for a pretest and the other, for a posttest.

If a student misses the first two words of a group and it is apparent that the words are too difficult, discontinue testing in that group. Remember that the purpose of the Check Test is simply to identify specific skill deficits and to determine a starting point for instruction. Do not unnecessarily frustrate the student. In some cases, you may wish to administer the Check Test in sections as the students progress through the book rather than in one sitting.

INTERPRETING RESULTS AND PLANNING INSTRUCTION

Record the students' Check Test results on the Accuracy Checklists. A blank Accuracy Checklist is provided on page 69 and at the back of the student's workbook. Record section scores in reading and spelling as a fraction, writing the number read or spelled correctly over the number five. Refer to the sample Accuracy Checklist on page 5.

By examining the Check Test Scores column, it should be readily apparent which list a student should begin work on. If a student reads and spells all words from a particular section correctly, instruction on the corresponding list is not necessary and it can be marked "mastered." In this case, the student can immediately begin to build reading proficiency on that list (Step 6). If a student indicates mastery in reading but not in spelling, proceed through the learning steps that focus on the spelling tasks. If a student scores 4/5 for a given list, begin instruction at Step 5, working to increase accuracy. The accuracy check will reveal whether additional instruction on Steps 1 through 4 will be necessary. Obviously a student who reads or spells fewer than three words correctly will require more instructional time than a student who has nearly mastered that list.

LIST 34: UNACCENTED *i* = /ə/ OR /ĭ/

-i- = /ə/	*-i-* = /ə/	*-i-* = /ə/	*-ity* = /ə tē/	*-ity* = /ə tē/	*-ical* = /ĭ kəl/
* accident	* principal	magnificent	* ability	popularity	* chemical
* American	* principle	magnitude	* activity	possibility	* critical
* animal	* sensitive	manicure	* authority	publicity	* economical
* aptitude	* significant	meditate	* electricity	purity	* electrical
* article	* similar	Mexican	* majority	rapidity	* historical
* candidate	* substitute	monitor	* necessity	reliability	* medical
* capital	acquisitive	multitude	* personality	sanity	* musical
* citizen	altitude	optimist	* quality	sensibility	* political
* comparison	arbitrate	original	* quantity	severity	* practical
* compliment	artifact	pedicure	* reality	sincerity	* vertical
* continent	Baltimore	pessimist	* security	stupidity	clerical
* criminal	cannibal	prominent	* unity	vanity	comical
* difficult	captivate	ridicule	* university	vicinity	fanatical
* estimate	cardigan	sentiment	* varsity		geographical
* gratitude	carnival	solitude	annuity		grammatical
* hesitate	centipede	subsidy	capability		identical
* institute	certificate	unicorn	capacity		logical
* intelligent	detriment	uniform	captivity		methodical
* investigate	Florida	universe	cavity		nautical
* medicine	helicopter	venison	clarity		physical
* notify	hurricane	ventilate	dignity		radical
* officer	impediment	vertigo	entity		statistical
* participate	inhabitant		humanity		surgical
* politics	intimate		humidity		technical
* predicate	latitude		intensity		theatrical
* president	longitude		objectivity		typical

*Practical spelling words. The teacher and student should decide together how many of these words the student will be responsible for spelling.

CONCEPTS

Introduce:

Unaccented i as /ə/ — *i* in a middle syllable usually says /ə/ if it is surrounded by consonants *(similar, president)*. In some regions this unaccented *i* may be pronounced /ĭ/, but for simplicity we have listed it as /ə/ in the workbook. Alternative sounds of the unaccented *i* (/ē/ and /y/) are presented in Lists 35 and 36, respectively.

-ity as /ə tē/ — *-ity* is a common ending containing unaccented *i* as /ə/. It is found at the end of abstract nouns and always follows the accented syllable *(qual´ i ty, ac tiv´ i ty, per son al´ i ty)*.

-ical as /i kəl/ — *-ical* is a common ending containing the suffixes *-ic* and *-ical*. It is found at the end of adjectives and always follows the accented syllable *(prac´ ti cal, me chan´ i cal, ec o nom´ i cal)*.

Accent in words with unaccented i — The accent falls on the syllable just before unaccented *i*.

Review:

Middle-syllable schwa — The schwa sound is always found in unaccented syllables. Any vowel can make the schwa sound. *Megawords 3,* List 17, has examples of middle-syllable schwa spelled by vowels other than *i*. *Relative, enemy, chocolate,* and *singular* are examples of middle-syllable *a, e, o,* and *u* with a schwa sound.

LEARNING STEPS

STEP 1. Work with the Isolated Word Parts

Reading — The students will correctly identify unaccented *i* as schwa and pronounce syllables that contain unaccented *i*. (See Worksheet 34–A.)

Spelling — The students will spell dictated syllables that contain unaccented *i* as schwa. (See Worksheet 34–B.)

Dictate the following syllables and examples for Worksheet 34–B. Pronounce unaccented *i* as /ə/ or /ĭ/.

1. ri as in *hurricane*
2. pli as in *compliment*
3. fi as in *difficult*
4. ni as in *dignity*
5. di as in *candidate*
6. ti as in *continent*
7. bi as in *arbitrate*
8. sti as in *institute*
9. ci as in *principal*
10. ci as in *university*

STEP 2. Work with the Combined Word Parts

Reading — The students will practice accent patterns as they pronounce detached syllables and then combine them to read a whole word. (See Worksheets 34–C, 34–D, 34–E, and 34–F.)

Note: When *-ity* or *-ical* is added to the end of a word, the accent pattern changes *(a´ ble → a bil´ i ty)*. As a result, the first vowel sometimes has a schwa sound even though it appears in an open syllable.

Spelling — The students will isolate, pronounce, and spell syllables in words with unaccented *i* as schwa. (See Worksheets 34–G, 34–H, 34–I, and 34–J.)

Dictate slowly the following words for Worksheet 34–G. Make certain that the students repeat the word *(universe)*, isolate the missing syllables *(u, verse)*, and say them aloud while spelling.

1. capital
2. universe
3. quality
4. aptitude
5. reality
6. critical
7. authority
8. candidate
9. substitute
10. majority
11. electrical
12. security
13. president
14. historical
15. investigate
16. personality

STEP 3. Work with the Whole Word

Reading — The students will syllabify words and work with accent patterns. (See Worksheets 34–K and 34–L.)

Spelling — The students will practice spelling words from List 34. (See Worksheets 34–M and 34–N).

Dictate the following practical spelling words for Worksheet 34–N. Make certain that the students repeat the words and sound each syllable aloud while spelling.

1. president	2. personality	3. practical	4. American	5. vertical
6. quality	7. notify	8. authority	9. historical	10. sensitive
11. citizen	12. political	13. similar	14. electricity	15. estimate
16. substitute	17. activity	18. candidate	19. economical	20. animal

STEP 4. Work with Words in Context

Meaning — The students will use List 34 words in definitions and in context. (See Worksheets 34–O and 34–P.)

Reading and Spelling — The students will read and write sentences that contain List 34 words. (See Worksheet 34–Q.)

Note: Any words that exemplify the principles of the word list may be circled.

STEP 5. Increase Reading and Spelling Accuracy and Monitor Progress

Reading — The students will read ten randomly selected words from List 34 with 90 percent accuracy. Record their progress on the Accuracy Checklists.

Spelling — The students will spell from dictation ten practical spelling words from List 34 with 90 percent accuracy. Record their progress on the Accuracy Checklists.

STEP 6. Build Reading Proficiency, Monitor Progress, and Encourage Spontaneous Writing

Record students' progress on the Proficiency Graphs.

LIST 35: UNACCENTED *i* = /ē/ AND UNACCENTED *u*

-i- = /ē/	*-i-* = /ē/	*-i-* = /ē/	*-i-* = /ē/	*-u-*	*-u-*
* appreciate	accordion	experience	premium	* actual	educator
* appropriate	alleviate	exterior	radial	* annual	executive
* audience	aquarium	glorious	radiant	* casual	factual
* curious	auditorium	greedier	radiate	* continual	fluctuate
* custodian	aviation	happier	radiator	* continuous	fraudulent
* editorial	barbarian	humiliate	recipient	* document	graduate
* furious	calcium	illustrious	retaliate	* gradual	graduation
* idiot	cardiac	imperial	serial	* particular	individual
* immediate	centennial	industrious	sodium	* popular	manual
* industrial	champion	ingredient	solarium	* punctual	monument
* inferior	chariot	magnesium	studio	* ridiculous	mortuary
* librarian	colonial	malaria	suburbia	* singular	mutual
* material	condominium	maniac	tedious	* usual	perpetual
* medium	congenial	median	tedium	* visual	punctuate
* memorial	delirium	mediate	trivia	actuate	sensuous
* obedient	deteriorate	melodious	trivial	ambiguous	situate
* obvious	deviate	miniature	zodiac	articulate	spatula
* previous	diphtheria	mysterious		congratulate	stimulant
* radio	dubious	obedience		conspicuous	strenuous
* serious	emporium	opium		contemptuous	tarantula
* stadium	enthusiasm	oriole		corpulent	tuberculosis
* superior	enthusiastic	phobia		curriculum	vacuum
* various	envious	portfolio		educate	
	expedient	precarious		education	

*Practical spelling words. The teacher and student should decide together how many of these words the student will be responsible for spelling.

CONCEPTS

Introduce:

Unaccented i as /ē/ — *i* often says /ē/ when it is part of a middle syllable that precedes a syllable beginning with a vowel *(ob vi ous, li brar i an)*. Alternative sounds of unaccented *i* are presented in List 34 (*i* as /ə/, the most common pattern) and in List 36 (*i* as /y/).

Unaccented u — *u* in the middle syllable of a multisyllabic word is pronounced differently in various parts of the United States.
Dictionaries use the following to represent the sound: /ə/, /o͞o/, /yə/, /yo͞o/, or /ū/.

-t- as /ch/ — In unaccented middle syllables with *tu*, *t* says /ch/ as in *situate.*

-d- as /j/ — In unaccented middle syllables with *du*, *d* says /j/ as in *gradual.*

Note: In a few words with *-t-* as /ch/ and *-d-* as /j/, *t* or *d* technically ends the syllable before unaccented *u*. *Megawords 7* does not discuss this point. *Grad-u-ate, sit-u-ate,* and *ed-u-cate* may be divided *gra-du-ate, si-tu-ate,* and *e-du-cate* by some students on Worksheets 35–J and 35–K. Give credit for either answer.

Common endings with unaccented *i* and unaccented *u*:

- *-ial* says /ē əl/ *(radial)*
- *-ious* says /ē əs/ *(serious)*
- *-iate* says /ē āt/ *(radiate)*
- *-ual* says /ū əl/ *(gradual)*

Most of the List 35 words contain two or three vowels in a row. Students should not mistake the unaccented vowel and the vowel that follows it for a double-vowel pattern. Students must learn that the unaccented vowel usually ends one syllable and the following vowel begins the next syllable.

Dictionaries and textbooks offer various pronunciations for some List 35 words. Some dictionaries give unaccented *i* a short-*i* sound *(triv ĭ al, de lir ĭ um, ex ter ĭ or)*. However, many dictionaries and most people we consulted give the *i* an /ē/ sound. The sound may vary from region to region, and teachers should use whatever is appropriate for their area. In some words the unaccented *i* may be pronounced either /ē/ or /y/ *(congenial, Pennsylvania, warrior)*.

LEARNING STEPS

STEP 1. Work with the Isolated Word Parts

Reading — The students will correctly identify the following common endings:

- *-ial* as /ē əl/
- *-ious* as /ē əs/
- *-iate* as /ē āt/
- *-ual* as /ū əl/

The students will correctly identify unaccented *i* as /ē/ and unaccented *u* and pronounce them. (See Worksheet 35–A.)

Spelling — The students will spell dictated syllables that contain unaccented *i* as /ē/ and unaccented *u*. (See Worksheet 35–B.)

Dictate the following syllables and examples for Worksheet 35–B.

1. ni as in *maniac*
2. di as in *studio*
3. ci as in *appreciate*
4. vi as in *obvious*
5. bi as in *phobia*
6. tri as in *industrial*
7. mi as in *premium*
8. i as in *furious*
9. li as in *portfolio*
10. pi as in *opium*

STEP 2. Work with the Combined Word Parts

***Reading* —** The students will pronounce detached syllables and then combine them to read a whole word. The students will practice accent patterns. (See Worksheet 35–C.)

***Spelling* —** The students will isolate, pronounce, and spell syllables in words with unaccented *i* as /ē/. (See Worksheets 35–D, 35–E, 35–F, 35–G, 35–H, and 35–I.)

Dictate slowly the following words for Worksheet 35–D. Make certain that the students repeat the word *(radiator)*, isolate the missing syllables *(ra, a)*, and say them aloud while spelling.

1. trivia	2. sodium	3. radiator	4. superior	5. opium
6. immediate	7. custodian	8. envious	9. humiliate	10. congenial
11. popular	12. monument	13. congratulate	14. annual	15. usual
16. ridiculous				

STEP 3. Work with the Whole Word

***Reading* —** The students will syllabify words and work with accent patterns. (See Worksheets 35–J, 35–K, and 35–L.)

***Spelling* —** The students will practice spelling words from List 35. (See Worksheets 35–M, 35–N, and 35–O.)

Dictate the following practical spelling words for Worksheet 35–N. Slightly stress the significant feature (ending or unaccented *i* or *u*) of each word. Make certain that the students repeat the words and sound each syllable aloud while spelling.

1. previous	2. casual	3. memorial	4. immediate	5. stadium
6. document	7. material	8. visual	9. medium	10. continual
11. obvious	12. industrial	13. particular	14. popular	15. various
16. appreciate	17. serious	18. superior	19. singular	20. usual
21. inferior	22. actual			

STEP 4. Work with Words in Context

***Meaning* —** The students will use List 35 words in definitions and in context. (See Worksheets 35–P and 35–Q.)

***Reading and Spelling* —** The students will read and write sentences that contain List 35 words. (See Worksheet 35–R.)

Note: Any words that exemplify the principles of the word list may be circled.

STEP 5. Increase Reading and Spelling Accuracy and Monitor Progress

***Reading* —** The students will read ten randomly selected words from List 35 with 90 percent accuracy. Record their progress on the Accuracy Checklists.

Spelling — The students will spell from dictation ten practical spelling words from List 35 with 90 percent accuracy. Record their progress on the Accuracy Checklists.

STEP 6. Build Reading Proficiency, Monitor Progress, and Encourage Spontaneous Writing

Record students' progress on the Proficiency Graphs.

LIST 36: UNACCENTED *i* = /y/

* alien
* brilliant
* companion
* convenient
* familiar
* genius
* inconvenient
* Italian
* junior
* million
* onion
* opinion
* peculiar
* senior
* union

Australian
auxiliary
battalion
begonia
billiards
billion
Brazilian
bunion
civilian
communion
congenial
convenience
cotillion
dahlia
Daniel

dominion
gardenia
ingenious
leniency
lenient
magnolia
medallion
memorabilia
Nathaniel
Ophelia
paraphernalia
Pennsylvania
petunia
rebellion
rebellious

Spaniard
spaniel
stallion
valiant
Virginia
William

*Practical spelling words. The teacher and student should decide together how many of these words the student will be responsible for spelling.

CONCEPTS

Introduce:

***Unaccented i = /y/* —** *i* usually says /y/ when it is in an unaccented syllable and is preceded by *l* or *n* (*million*, *convenient*). When *i* says /y/, it is usually in an unaccented syllable at the end of a word. The accent is on the syllable *just before* the final syllable.

Review:

***Unaccented i = /ə/ or /ĭ/* —** *i* in an unaccented middle syllable usually has the schwa sound, /ə/, as in *similar* and *president*.

***Unaccented i = /ē/* —** In some words *i* in an unaccented middle syllable says /ē/ (*serious*, *material*). In such cases the *i* comes just before a final syllable that begins with a vowel.

LEARNING STEPS

STEP 1. Work with the Isolated Word Parts

***Reading* —** The students will correctly identify and pronounce syllables that contain unaccented *i* as /y/. (See Worksheet 36–A.)

***Spelling* —** The students will correctly spell dictated syllables that contain unaccented *i* as /y/. (See Worksheet 36–B.)

Dictate the following syllables and examples after reviewing the key on Worksheet 36–B. The second acceptable choice is in parentheses.

1. -ion as in *million* (ian)
2. -ia as in *petunia*
3. -ial as in *congenial* (iel)
4. -ior as in *senior* (iar)
5. -iant as in *valiant* (ient)
6. -iel as in *Daniel* (-ial)
7. -ion as in *onion* (-ian)
8. -ient as in *lenient* (-iant)
9. -ia as in *Virginia*
10. -iar as in *familiar* (-ior)

STEP 2. Work with the Combined Word Parts

***Reading* —** The students will pronounce detached syllables and then combine them to read a whole word. The students will practice accent patterns. (See Worksheet 36–C.)

***Spelling* —** The students will isolate, pronounce, and spell syllables in words with unaccented *i* as /y/. (See Worksheets 36–D, 36–E, and 36–F.)

Dictate slowly the following words for Worksheet 36–D. Make certain that the students repeat the word *(companion),* isolate the missing syllables *(com, ion),* and say them aloud while spelling.

1. bunion	2. companion	3. opinion	4. dominion	5. senior
6. junior	7. lenient	8. inconvenient	9. convenient	10. Virginia
11. petunia	12. magnolia	13. civilian	14. Italian	15. Brazilian

STEP 3. Work with the Whole Word

***Reading* —** The students will syllabify words, practice accent patterns, and discriminate between words with unaccented *i as /y/* and unaccented *i as /ē/*. (See Worksheets 36–G and 36–H.)

***Spelling* —** The students will practice spelling words from List 36. (See Worksheet 36–I.)

Dictate the following practical spelling words for Worksheet 36–I. Make certain that the students repeat the words and sound each syllable aloud while spelling.

1. onion	2. junior	3. convenient	4. opinion	5. peculiar
6. senior	7. Italian	8. million	9. brilliant	10. union
11. familiar	12. companion	13. behavior		

STEP 4. Work with Words in Context

Meaning **—** The students will use List 36 words in definitions and in context. (See Worksheets 36–J and 36–K.)

Reading and Spelling **—** The students will read and write sentences that contain List 36 words. (See Worksheet 36–L.)

Note: Any words that exemplify the principles of the word list may be circled.

STEP 5. Increase Reading and Spelling Accuracy and Monitor Progress

Reading **—** The students will read ten randomly selected words from List 36 with 90 percent accuracy. Record their progress on the Accuracy Checklists.

Spelling **—** The students will spell from dictation ten practical spelling words from List 36 with 90 percent accuracy. Record their progress on the Accuracy Checklists.

STEP 6. Build Reading Proficiency, Monitor Progress, and Encourage Spontaneous Writing

Record students' progress on the Proficiency Graphs.

LIST 37: *ti* AND *ci* ENDINGS

-cial	*-tial*	*-cious*	*-tious*	*-cient, -tient, -cience, -tience*
* artificial	* essential	* conscious	* ambitious	* ancient
* especially	* partial	* delicious	* cautious	* efficient
* financial	* potential	* precious	* nutritious	* patience
* judicial	* presidential	* suspicious	fictitious	* patient
* official	* residential	* unconscious	flirtatious	* quotient
* racial	confidential	atrocious	infectious	conscience
* social	credential	audacious	scrumptious	deficient
* special	impartial	auspicious	superstitious	omniscient
beneficial	initial	fallacious		proficient
commercial	martial	ferocious		sufficient
crucial	nuptial	gracious		
facial	sequential	judicious		
glacial	spatial	luscious		
provincial	substantial	malicious		
		precocious		
		spacious		
		specious		
		tenacious		
		vicious		

*Practical spelling words. The teacher and student should decide together how many of these words the student will be responsible for spelling.

CONCEPTS

Introduce:

ti and ci Endings — *ti* and *ci* often combine with *al*, *ous*, *ent*, and *ence* to form final syllables in words (*social*, *partial*, *delicious*, *cautious*, *ancient*, *patient*, *conscience*, *patience*). When this happens, *ti* and *ci* say /sh/. As in words that end in *tion* and *cian*, the accent is *always* on the syllable that comes *just before ti* and *ci (pa´ tient, in fec´ tious, con fi den´ tial).*

LEARNING STEPS

STEP 1. Work with the Isolated Word Parts

Reading — The students will correctly identify and pronounce the isolated endings *-cial*, *-tial*, *-cious*, *-tious*, *-cient*, *-tient*, *-cience* and *-tience*. (See Worksheet 37–A.)

Spelling — The students will generate spellings for the *ti* and *ci* endings. (See Worksheet 37–B.)

STEP 2. Work with the Combined Word Parts

Reading — The students will practice accent patterns as they pronounce detached syllables and then combine them to read a whole word. (See Worksheets 37–C, 37–D, and 37–E.)

Spelling — The students will isolate, pronounce, and spell syllables in words that contain *ti* and *ci* endings. (See Worksheets 37–F, 37–G, and 37–H.)

Dictate the following words for Worksheet 37–H. Make certain that the students repeat the word (*unconscious*), isolate the missing syllables *(un, cious),* and say them aloud while spelling.

1. facial	2. spacious	3. special	4. patient	5. initial
6. ancient	7. unconscious	8. financial	9. substantial	10. nutritious
11. artificial	12. ambitious	13. sequential	14. especially	15. delicious
16. superstitious				

STEP 3. Work with the Whole Word

Reading — The students will syllabify words, practice accent patterns, and identify the accented syllable and the *ti* or *ci* ending. (See Worksheets 37–I and 37–J.)

Spelling — The students will practice spelling words from List 37. (See Worksheets 37–K and 37–L.)

Dictate the following practical spelling words for Worksheet 37–L. Make certain that the students repeat the words and sound each syllable aloud while spelling.

1. social	2. cautious	3. conscious	4. ancient	5. special
6. especially	7. patient	8. racial	9. precious	10. essential
11. ambitious	12. quotient	13. official	14. delicious	15. presidential
16. judicial	17. residential	18. financial	19. nutritious	20. efficient

STEP 4. Work with Words in Context

Meaning — The students will use List 37 words in definitions and in context. (See Worksheets 37–M and 37–N.)

Reading and Spelling — The students will read and write sentences that contain List 37 words. (See Worksheet 37–O.)

Note: Any words that exemplify the principles of the word list may be circled.

STEP 5. Increase Reading and Spelling Accuracy and Monitor Progress

Reading — The students will read ten randomly selected words from List 37 with 90 percent accuracy. Record their progress on the Accuracy Checklists.

Spelling — The students will spell from dictation ten practical spelling words from List 37 with 90 percent accuracy. Record their progress on the Accuracy Checklists.

STEP 6. Build Reading Proficiency, Monitor Progress, and Encourage Spontaneous Writing

Record students' progress on the Proficiency Graphs.

LIST 38: ADVANCED V/V COMBINATIONS

/ē/

* cereal
* geography
* hideous
* ideal
* museum
* reaction
* reality
* realize
* reappear
* reunion
* stereo
* theater
* theory
* video

cameo
creation
delineate
geology
geometry
linear
meander
meteor
Minneapolis
neon
nucleus
permeate
preamble
reinforce

/ī/

* anxiety
* client
* dialect
* science
* trial
* variety
* violate
* violence
* violent

biology
bionic
defiant
denial
diagram
diamond
diary
iodine
iota
piety
pioneer
priority
reliance
riotous
triumphant
vial
violation
violet
violin

/ō/

* cooperate
* coordination
* poetry

boa
coagulate
coagulation
coeducation
coerce
coercion
cooperation
coordinate
oasis
poetic
stoic
zoology

/ā/

chaos
chaotic

/ū/ and /o͞o/

* annual
* cruelty
* fluent
* fluid
* graduate
* truant

altruism
altruistic
ambiguity
annuity
biannual
congruent
continuous
continuum
dual
duel
fluency
influence
influential
influenza
minuet
truancy

*Practical spelling words. The teacher and student should decide together how many of these words the student will be responsible for spelling.

CONCEPTS

Introduce:

The V/V Division Rule — If two vowels together do not make a recognizable word when sounded as a double vowel, divide between the vowels. The second vowel starts the next syllable (*re ac tion*, *in flu en tial*).

Some of the words in List 38 were previously introduced in *Megawords 1*, List 8, in which simple V/V words were presented. They are included here to increase the word pool and to provide easy examples of the V/V concept. Some V/V words with *u* were previously discussed in List 35, in which unaccented *u* and *i* were presented.

Review:

Double-Vowel Patterns — Certain double-vowel groupings can be pronounced as double vowels or as V/V (*ea* in *bread* or *cre ate*, *oe* in *woe* or *po e try*). Students should be encouraged to be flexible when encountering such words—if one way doesn't work, try the other. V/V combinations presented here are ones in which the first vowel has its own long sound. Lists 35 and 36 discussed *i* as /ē/ (*opium*) and *i* as /y/ (*junior*).

LEARNING STEPS

STEP 1. Work with the Isolated Word Parts

Reading — The students will correctly identify and pronounce syllables with V/V combinations. (See Worksheet 38–A.)

Drill cards using syllables such as those in Worksheet 38–A might be helpful. They should be keyed so that the students know to give the V/V pronunciation rather than a double-vowel pronunciation.

Spelling — The students will spell dictated syllables that include V/V combinations. (See Worksheet 38–A.)

Dictate the following syllables and examples for Worksheet 38–A.

1. teor as in *meteor*
2. *io as in iodine*
3. ual as in *annual*
4. ium as in *triumphant*
5. ience as in *science*
6. eo as in *cameo*
7. dia as in *dialect*
8. ial as in *denial*
9. uence as in *influence*
10. coag as in *coagulation*

Variant spellings for the schwa sound should be allowed at this point (*ience* or *iance*, etc.).

STEP 2. Work with the Combined Word Parts

Reading — The students will pronounce detached syllables and combine them to read a whole word. The students will practice accent patterns. (See Worksheet 38–B.)

Spelling — The students will practice spelling syllables heard in words with V/V combinations. (See Worksheets 38–C, 38–D, 38–E, and 38–F.)

Dictate the following words for Worksheet 38–C. Make certain that the students repeat the word (*diagram*), isolate the missing syllables *(di, gram),* and say them aloud while spelling.

1. trial
2. fluid
3. diagram
4. ideal
5. violet
6. iodine
7. reaction
8. cereal
9. reliance
10. zoology
11. cooperation
12. influential
13. graduate
14. reinforce
15. poetry
16. altruistic

STEP 3. Work with the Whole Word

Reading — The students will syllabify words, practice accent patterns, and discriminate between V/V and double-vowel words. (See Worksheets 38–G, 38–H, and 38–I.)

***Spelling* —** The students will practice spelling words from List 38. (See Worksheets 38–J and 38–K.)

Dictate the following practical spelling words for Worksheet 38–K. Make certain that the students repeat the words and sound each syllable aloud while spelling.

1. poetry	2. science	3. cruelty	4. ideal	5. realize
6. museum	7. client	8. variety	9. coordinate	10. truant
11. fluid	12. annual	13. graduate	14. going	15. fluent
16. cooperate	17. trial	18. diary	19. hideous	20. theater

STEP 4. Work with Words in Context

***Meaning* —** The students will use List 38 words in definitions and in context. (See Worksheets 38–L and 38–M.)

***Reading and Spelling* —** The students will read and write sentences that contain List 38 words. (See Worksheet 38–N.)

Note: Any words that exemplify the principles of the word list may be circled.

STEP 5. Increase Reading and Spelling Accuracy and Monitor Progress

***Reading* —** The students will read ten randomly selected words from List 38 with 90 percent accuracy. Record their progress on the Accuracy Checklists.

***Spelling* —** The students will spell from dictation ten practical spelling words from List 38 with 90 percent accuracy. Record their progress on the Accuracy Checklists.

STEP 6. Build Reading Proficiency, Monitor Progress, and Encourage Spontaneous Writing

Record students' progress on the Proficiency Graphs.

REVIEW LISTS 34–38

* accident	* junior	* unconscious	greedier	reaction
* alien	* medical	* video	humidity	reality
* ambitious	* million	ancient	hurricane	reappear
* American	* museum	atrocious	inferior	rebellion
* animal	* nutritious	auditorium	latitude	reunion
* annual	* official	begonia	lenient	riotous
* artificial	* onion	captivity	librarian	serious
* brilliant	* opinion	carnival	martial	solitude
* cautious	* poetry	chaotic	meander	stoicism
* companion	* potential	chariot	medium	trivial
* convenient	* precious	chemical	miniature	truant
* cooperate	* previous	coerce	musical	unicorn
* delicious	* radio	commercial	necessity	variety
* especially	* residential	compliment	noxious	varsity
* essential	* science	denial	obvious	vertical
* familiar	* senior	diary	participate	vertigo
* financial	* singular	difficult	petunia	vicious
* genius	* social	document	pneumonia	violent
* geography	* stadium	gardenia	preamble	Virginia
* immediate	* suspicious	graduate	punctual	William

*Practical spelling words. The teacher and student should decide together how many of these words the student will be responsible for spelling.

LEARNING STEPS

For the Review List, only Steps 5 and 6 are applicable.

STEP 5. Increase Reading and Spelling Accuracy and Monitor Progress

***Reading* —** The students will read ten randomly selected words from the Review List with 90 percent accuracy. Record their progress on the Accuracy Checklists.

***Spelling* —** The students will spell from dictation ten practical spelling words from the Review List with 90 percent accuracy. Record their progress on the Accuracy Checklists.

STEP 6. Build Reading Proficiency, Monitor Progress, and Encourage Spontaneous Writing

Record students' progress on the Proficiency Graphs.

The optional crossword puzzle provides a cumulative review of words from *Megawords 1–7*. Because it is substantially more difficult than other puzzles in *Megawords*, you may find it helpful to have the whole class or a group of students work on it (with your assistance when necessary).

WORKSHEET 34–A

i in an unaccented middle syllable usually has the schwa sound, /ə/ (*similar, president*).[1]

Circle the syllables that contain unaccented *i* in the following words.

ar (bi) trate	cap (i) tal	pol (i) tics	ven (i) son
an (i) mal	pred (i) cate	mon (i) tor	ar (ti) fact
det (ri) ment	mul (ti) tude	sol (i) tude	pres (i) dent
u (ni) form	op (ti) mist	sub (sti) tute	ac (ci) dent
ap (ti) tude	sen (si) tive	u (ni) corn	prom (i) nent

Where is the syllable that contains *i*? in the middle syllable

i often combines with one or two consonants to form a syllable. Even though the syllable ends in a vowel, it has a schwa sound rather than a long-vowel sound. Pronounce these syllables that contain unaccented *i*, giving *i* the schwa sound.

ti	sti	ci	ni	ri
bi	di	si	pli	fi

-ity, pronounced /ə tē/, is a common ending in which *i* says /ə/.
-ical, pronounced /ĭ kəl/, is a common ending that contains the suffixes *-ic* and *-al*. *i* has its short sound in this ending.

Circle and pronounce the endings *-ity* and *-ical* in the words below.

clar(ity)	polit(ical)	humid(ity)	possibil(ity)	phys(ical)
geograph(ical)	necess(ity)	techn(ical)	chem(ical)	activ(ity)
maj(ority)	vicin(ity)	mechan(ical)	intens(ity)	naut(ical)

Review: *i* in an unaccented middle syllable usually says / ə /.

Two common endings in which *i* says /ə/ or /ĭ/ are -ity and -ical.

[1] *i* has two other sounds in unaccented middle syllables. *i* pronounced /ē/ (*radial*) is discussed in List 35. *i* pronounced /y/ (*million*) is discussed in List 36.

WORKSHEET 34–B

Review: Unaccented *i* is often found in the middle syllable of multisyllabic words. It most often has a schwa sound.

Your teacher will dictate some syllables that contain *i* pronounced /ə/. Say the syllable aloud as you write it, spelling the schwa sound *i*.

1. ri	4. ni	6. ti	8. sti
2. pli	5. di	7. bi	9. ci
3. fi			10. si

How do you spell the ending pattern pronounced /ə tē/? ity

How do you spell the ending pattern pronounced /ĭ kəl/? ical

Circle and write the middle syllable that contains unaccented *i* in the following words. It will be one of the ten syllables that you spelled above.

ar(ti)cle	ti	can(ni)bal	ni
com(pli)ment	pli	ar(bi)trate	bi
sub(si)dy	si	prin(ci)ple	ci
of(fi)cer	fi	hur(ri)cane	ri
sub(sti)tute	sti	car(di)gan	di

Unscramble these multisyllabic words.

verse ni u	universe	tive sen si	sensitive
cal ti ver	vertical	i med cal	medical
tude i sol	solitude	i da Flor	Florida
tal cap i	capital	ty ni dig	dignity
hes tate i	hesitate	dent ac ci	accident
hur cane ri	hurricane	u form ni	uniform

WORKSHEET 34–C

i is not the only vowel that can spell the schwa sound. Any unaccented vowel can have the schwa sound. Review *Megawords 3*, List 17, in which *a, e, o* and *u* have the schwa sound. When you spell, learn to try another vowel if one does not look right.

Circle the unaccented middle syllable in each word. Then write the words in the correct column as shown.

sub (sti) tute	rel (a) tive	dif (fi) cult	per (ma) nent
cus (to) mer	el (e) phant	por (cu) pine	al (co) hol
of (fi) cer	com (pro) mise	ben (e) fit	sep (a) rate
en (e) my			reg (u) lar

a Says /ə/	*e* Says /ə/	*i* Says /ə/
relative	enemy	substitute
permanent	elephant	officer
separate	benefit	difficult

o Says /ə/	*u* Says /ə/
customer	porcupine
compromise	regular
alcohol	

Cover the top half of this page and fill in the vowel that spells the schwa sound in the practical spelling words below.

rel_a_tive	reg_u_lar	porc_u_pine
ben_e_fit	diff_i_cult	alc_o_hol
sep_a_rate	perm_a_nent	cust_o_mer
el_e_phant	compr_o_mise	en_e_my
arg_u_ment	subst_i_tute	off_i_cer

Now uncover the page and check your work.

WORKSHEET 34–D

A syllable in which *i* says /ə/ is never accented. The accent is on the syllable *just before* it. The accented syllable is pronounced as if it were a one-syllable word, having a short, long, *r*-controlled, or double-vowel sound.

Circle the syllables that contain unaccented *i*. Draw a box around the accented syllable just before the syllable with unaccented *i*. Then pronounce and combine the syllables to read the whole word.

[sim] (i) lar	similar	sig [nif] (i) cant	significant
[prom] (i) nent	prominent	[in] (sti) tute	institute
im [ped] (i) ment	impediment	cer [tif] (i) cate	certificate
ac [quis] (i) tive	acquisitive	[ar] (bi) trate	arbitrate
[pes] (si) mist	pessimist	[no] (ti) fy	notify
in [ves] (ti) gate	investigate	mag [nif] (i) cent	magnificent
[in] (ti) mate	intimate	[com] (pli) ment	compliment
[tes] (ti) mo ny	testimony	[u] (ni) verse	universe
[u] (ni) form	uniform	in [tel] (li) gent	intelligent

-ity		*-ical*	
[dig] (ni) ty	dignity	[prac] (ti) cal	practical
[cav] (i) ty	cavity	[com] (i) cal	comical
[san] (i) ty	sanity	[crit] (i) cal	critical
hu [mid] (i) ty	humidity	i [den] (ti) cal	identical
se [cur] (i) ty	security	his [tor] (i) cal	historical
a [bil] (i) ty	ability	e [lec] (tri) cal	electrical
pos *si [bil] (i) ty	possibility	sta [tis] (ti) cal	statistical
pop u [lar] (i) ty	popularity	ge o [graph] (i) cal	geographical
u *ni [ver] (si) ty	university	ec o [nom] (i) cal	economical

*These syllables also contain unaccented *i*.

WORKSHEET 34–E

In most two- and three-syllable words, the accent is on the first syllable. However, when *-ity* or *-ical* is added to the end of a word, the accent pattern changes. The accent always falls on the syllable *just before -ity* and *-ical*.

Draw a box around the accented syllables. If the accented syllable has a long- or short-vowel sound, mark it as shown below. Then pronounce and combine the syllables.

Accent the First Syllable	Accent Just Before *-ity* or *-ical*
[rē] al	re [ăl] i ty
[stū] pid	stu [pĭd] i ty
[hū] man	hu [măn] i ty
[căp] tive	cap [tĭv] i ty
[hĭs] to ry	his [tor] i cal
[ăc] tive	ac [tĭv] i ty
[pŏl] i tics	po [lĭt] i cal
[per] son al	per son [ăl] i ty
[thē] a ter	the [ăt] ri cal
[pŏs] si ble	pos si [bĭl] i ty
[răp] id	ra [pĭd] i ty
[hū] mid	hu [mĭd] i ty
[mĕth] od	me [thŏd] i cal
[fĕs] tive	fes [tĭv] i ty
[sĕn] si ble	sen si [bĭl] i ty
[fī] nal	fi [năl] i ty
[pŏp] u lar	pop u [lar] i ty
[cā] pa ble	ca pa [bĭl] i ty
[pŭb] lic	pub [lĭc] i ty
[nā] tive	na [tĭv] i ty
[frăg] ile	fra [gĭl] i ty

WORKSHEET 34–F

Sometimes the accent in multisyllabic words is on the second syllable. When *-ity* or *-ical* is added to such words, the accent may either shift to another syllable or stay on the same syllable.

Draw a box around the accented syllables. If the accented syllable has a long- or short-vowel sound, mark it as shown below. Remember to accent the syllable *just before* an *-ity* or *-ical* ending. Then pronounce and combine the syllables. Read across. Check the Accent Shift column if the accent shifts to a new syllable.

Accent the Second Syllable	Accent Just Before *-ity* or *-ical*	Accent Shift
ob [jĕc] tive	ob jec [tĭv] i ty	✓
in [tĕnse]	in [tĕn] si ty	
e [lĕc] tric	e lec [trĭc] i ty	✓
e [cŏn] o my	ec o [nŏm] i cal	✓
i [dĕn] ti ty	i [dĕn] ti cal	
ge [ŏg] raph y	ge o [grăph] i cal	✓
e [lĕc] tric	e [lĕc] tri cal	
me [chăn] ic	me [chăn] i cal	
re [lī] a ble	re li a [bĭl] i ty	✓
se [cure]	se [cur] i ty	

In the following *er*V words, the sound of the vowel changes from /eer/ to /air/ when *-ity* is added.

sin cere	sin cer i ty
se vere	se ver i ty

Draw a box around the accented syllable in each word. Practice changing the accent pattern as you pronounce and combine the syllables in these words.

[nec] es sar y	ne [ces] si ty
ne [ces] si tate	nec es [sar] i ly

WORKSHEET 34–G

Your teacher will dictate some words with unaccented *i*. Sound out each word as you write the missing syllable(s). Then write the whole word, saying it aloud as you spell it.

	Copy	ABC Order
1. cap i tal	capital	aptitude
2. u ni verse	universe	authority
3. qual i ty	quality	candidate
4. ap ti tude	aptitude	capital
5. re al i ty	reality	critical
6. crit i cal	critical	electrical
7. au thor i ty	authority	historical
8. can di date	candidate	investigate
9. sub sti tute	substitute	majority
10. ma jor i ty	majority	personality
11. e lec tri cal	electrical	president
12. se cur i ty	security	quality
13. pres i dent	president	reality
14. his tor i cal	historical	security
15. in ves ti gate	investigate	substitute
16. per son al i ty	personality	universe

Now go back and write the words in alphabetical order.

Review: Accent the syllable before an *-ical* or *-ity* ending.

Syllables containing schwa *i* are never accented.

i in an unaccented middle syllable is most commonly pronounced /ə/. In the ending *-ical, i* is pronounced /ĭ/.

WORKSHEET 34–H

al is the most common way to spell the /əl/ sound at the end of three- and four-syllable words. Use the definitions to figure out the words below. Write the missing syllable using *al* and then write the whole word.

	Accented Syllable	Unaccented Syllable	*-al* Syllable	Copy
1. Opposite of horizontal	ver	ti	cal	vertical
2. Most important; the head of a school	prin	ci	pal	principal
3. A living thing that is not a plant	an	i	mal	animal
4. A city where the seat of government is	cap	i	tal	capital
5. A person guilty of a crime	crim	i	nal	criminal
6. A traveling show	car	ni	val	carnival
7. Someone who eats human flesh	can	ni	bal	cannibal

Use *ent* or *ant* to spell the /ənt/ sound at the end of words containing a middle syllable with an unaccented *i*. Use the definitions to figure out the missing syllable and then write the whole word.

		Add *ent*	Copy
8. The leader of a country	pres i	dent	president
9. North America, Europe, and Africa are examples	con ti	nent	continent
10. Well-known; easy to see	prom i	nent	prominent
11. Good at learning things	in tel li	gent	intelligent
12. An obstruction or hindrance	im ped i	ment	impediment
13. Splendid; grand	mag nif i	cent	magnificent
14. An unlucky happening	ac ci	dent	accident

		Add *ant*	Copy
15. Important	sig nif i	cant	significant
16. Person who lives in a place	in hab i	tant	inhabitant

WORKSHEET 34–I

/o͞o/ at the end of multisyllabic words is usually spelled as a silent-*e* syllable with *u*-consonant-*e*.

Add the final syllable *-tude* to these words with unaccented *i*.

*apti tude	multi tude	magni tude
lati tude	*grati tude	soli tude

Add the final syllable *-tute*.

*insti tute *substi tute

Match each word from above to its definition. Write the words by syllables on the lines below.

	Accented Syllable	Unaccented Syllable	VC*e* Syllable
1. Talent; ability	ap	ti	tude
2. The state of being solitary or alone	sol	i	tude
3. Take the place of another	sub	sti	tute
4. Distance north or south of the equator	lat	i	tude
5. Size; greatness	mag	ni	tude
6. A crowd	mul	ti	tude
7. An organization; a school	in	sti	tute
8. Thankfulness	grat	i	tude

Have another student test you on spelling the starred words. They are practical spelling words.

My score: ________words correct.

Three words that end in *itude* have to do with distance. Connect each word to its definition.

altitude	distance north or south of the equator
longitude	distance (or height) above sea level
latitude	distance east or west on the earth's surface

WORKSHEET 34–J

Use *ate* to spell /āt/ at the end of multisyllabic words. Use the definitions to figure out the words below. Write the missing syllable using *ate*, and then write the whole word.

		Accented Syllable	Unaccented Syllable	*ate* Syllable	Copy
1. To settle a dispute		ar	bi	trate	arbitrate
2. To hold back because of doubt		hes	i	tate	hesitate
3. A person who seeks office		can	di	date	candidate
4. To change or purify the air		ven	ti	late	ventilate
5. To charm; to influence with charm		cap	ti	vate	captivate
6. To make easier or help	fa	cil	i	tate	facilitate
7. To take part in	par	tic	i	pate	participate
8. To study or search into	in	ves	ti	gate	investigate

Sometimes ate is used to spell the /ət/ ending in multisyllabic words.

9. A document stating a fact	cer	tif	i	cate	certificate
10. Very personal; known very well		in	ti	mate	intimate
11. A rough calculation of how much or how many		es	ti	mate	estimate
12. The part of a sentence that contains the verb		pred	i	cate	predicate

Look at the words above.

Most of the words in which *ate* says /āt/ are verbs (adjectives, nouns, verbs).

Most of the words in which *ate* says /ət/ are nouns (adjectives, nouns, verbs).

WORKSHEET 34–K

In the following words, identify the syllables that contain unaccented *i*. Then copy the words by syllables under the correct heading, writing the accented syllables in the boxes. Mark the accented vowels and pronounce the words.

If the accented syllable has a short-vowel sound, it ends in a consonant.

If the accented syllable has a long-vowel sound, it ends in a vowel.

If the accented syllable has an *r*-controlled sound, it ends with the letter r.

	Accented Syllable	Unaccented Syllable	
centipede	cĕn	ti	pede
notify	nō	ti	fy
detriment	dĕt	ri	ment
ridicule	rĭd	i	cule
technical	tĕch	ni	cal
uniform	ū	ni	form

	Accented Syllable	Unaccented Syllable	
unicorn	ū	ni	corn
optimist	ŏp	ti	mist
unity	ū	ni	ty
manicure	măn	i	cure
universe	ū	ni	verse
vertigo	ver	ti	go

		Accented Syllable	Unaccented Syllable	
intelligent	in	tĕl	li	gent
necessity	ne	cĕs	si	ty
vicinity	vi	cĭn	i	ty
magnificent	mag	nĭf	i	cent
comparison	com	par	i	son

WORKSHEET 34–L

Identify the accented syllables. Then copy each word by syllables under the correct heading. Write the accented syllables in the boxes.

radical	electricity	geographical	popularity	reality
activity	artifact	subsidy	authority	economical
detriment	theatrical	objectivity	surgical	capability

Accent the First Syllable

rad	i	cal
det	ri	ment
ar	ti	fact
sub	si	dy
sur	gi	cal

Accent the Second Syllable

ac	tiv	i	ty
the	at	ri	cal
au	thor	i	ty
re	al	i	ty

Accent the Third Syllable

e	lec	tric	i	ty
ge	o	graph	i	cal
ob	jec	tiv	i	ty
pop	u	lar	i	ty
ec	o	nom	i	cal
cap	a	bil	i	ty

Review: The accented syllable always comes *just before* the syllable with unaccented *i*.

WORKSHEET 34–M

-ical is an adjective ending. Make adjectives out of these nouns by adding *ical*. Remember to apply the Drop-the-*e* Rule or the *Y* Rule when necessary. Use a dictionary to help you decide when to add, drop, or change some letters.

Noun Root + *ical* = Adjective

history	historical	method	methodical
identity	identical	geography	geographical
economy	economical	grammar	grammatical
practice	practical	surgery	surgical

-ity is a noun ending. Make nouns out of these adjectives by adding *ity*. Remember to apply the spelling rules. Use a dictionary to help you decide when to add, drop, or change some letters.

Adjective Root + *ity* = Noun

vain	vanity	personal	personality
sane	sanity	capable	capability
pure	purity	electric	electricity
clear	clarity	reliable	reliability
real	reality	fragile	fragility
final	finality	intense	intensity
public	publicity	sensible	sensibility

Proofing Practice: Two common List 34 words are misspelled in each of the sentences below. Correct them as shown.

1. Did you hear about the helicopter ~~accidant~~ accident at the carnival in ~~Baltamore~~ Baltimore?
2. Percival was ~~criticle~~ critical of the new ~~surgeoal~~ surgical institute and the medical school.
3. Is there any ~~posibility~~ possibility that Abigail will play on the ~~varsety~~ varsity team this fall?
4. It is ~~dificult~~ difficult to estimate the ~~severety~~ severity of the damage until we investigate.

WORKSHEET 34–N

Your teacher will dictate some practical spelling words from List 34. Say the words aloud as you write them under the correct heading.

Unaccented *i*	*-ity* Ending
president	personality
American	quality
notify	authority
sensitive	electricity
citizen	activity
similar	*-ical* Ending
estimate	practical
substitute	vertical
candidate	historical
animal	political
	economical

Find and circle the twenty words above in the puzzle below. The words can be found in a straight line across or up and down. Write the leftover letters in the blanks below.

P R E S I D E N T L Q E A R E L E C T R I C I T Y
O N S E I N G O S W U I P R A C T I C A L A T H V
L O T N U T T T I H A A M E R I C A N O U N G H E
I T I S I A N I M A L S U B S T I T U T E D S L R
T A M I B O R F I L I O A C T I V I T Y S I T T T
I H A T O U G Y L H T A U T H O R I T Y T D W I I
C I T I Z E N T A H Y E C O N O M I C A L A O U C
A T E V L E A R R P E R S O N A L I T Y N T I N A
L G I E S H I S T O R I C A L P E R I L O E U S L

LEARNING WITHOUT THOUGHT IS LABOR LOST; THOUGHT WITHOUT LEARNING IS PERILOUS. —CONFUCIUS

WORKSHEET 34–O

Fill in each blank with a word from below that makes sense in the sentence. Use a dictionary to look up unfamiliar words. Underline the phrase in each sentence that gives you a clue to the meaning of the following words.

optimist	principles	pedicure	vertigo	artifacts
pessimist	quality	venison	centipede	annuity
principal	unicorn	varsity	subsidy	quantity

1. The principal of our school had a firm belief that students should respect one another. The head of our school is a woman of high principles.
2. The technician experienced vertigo as she climbed higher up the ladder. She started to get dizzy, feeling as if she were whirling about.
3. Ms. Mortimer decided to get a pedicure. It was the first time she had ever had her toenails trimmed and polished when she was at the beauty salon.
4. It is important to look for quality rather than quantity when you shop for clothes. A few well-made outfits will serve you better than many poorly made items.
5. The single, long horn of the unicorn symbolizes purity and unity in the old myths.
6. Dolores was able to get a rent subsidy. Without the grant money she would have had to vacate her apartment.
7. Dominic made the varsity basketball team. With all the time he spent training, he deserved to make the top team.
8. Alison always looks on the bright side of things, but Percival is usually glum about life. It's much more pleasant to be around an optimist like Alison than a pessimist like Percival.
9. Venison is tougher than beef. Quite frankly, I don't care for deer meat.
10. Ms. Sheridan receives an annuity from her company. The sum of money is paid yearly.
11. Oliver jumped when he saw a wormlike insect with many legs in the bathtub. He didn't want to take a bath with a centipede!
12. There were many Navajo artifacts in the museum. The handmade articles were truly beautiful.

WORKSHEET 34–P

Listed below are words from List 34 that you are likely to use in writing. Be sure you learn how to spell these practical spelling words. Fill in each blank with a word that makes sense in the sentence. Then complete the puzzle.

difficult	necessity	intelligent	continent	hesitate
majority	ability	critical	participate	chemicals

1. Musical ability (2 Down) is often apparent at an early age.
2. Even though I study hard, algebra is a difficult (5 Across) subject for me.
3. A proper diet is a necessity (8 Across) for good health.
4. The United States is located on the continent (7 Across) of North America.
5. There are no chemicals (4 Down) or preservatives in this brand of ice cream.
6. The employees voted and a majority (9 Across) are in favor of the four-day work week.
7. Mr. Archibald did not approve of my plan to change jobs. In fact, he was rather critical (1 Down) of my decision.
8. Dolphins are intelligent (6 Across) mammals. They learn tricks easily.
9. I hope you won't hesitate (10 Across) to participate (3 Across) in our fund-raising campaign.

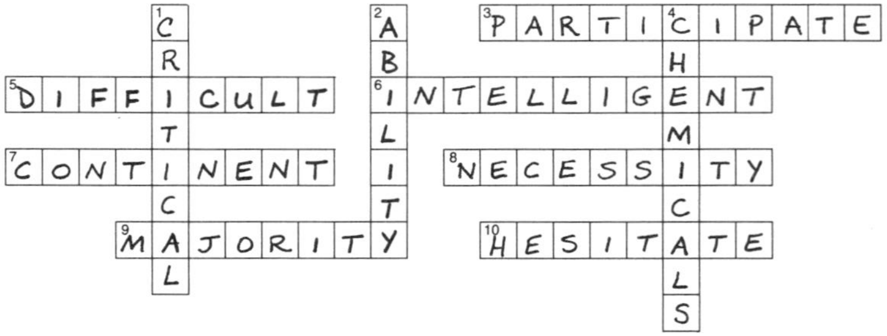

WORKSHEET 34–Q

Read the following sentences and circle all the List 34 words that you can find.

1. The majority of university students do not participate in political activities.
2. Emily received a similar estimate for electrical work from both contractors.
3. The P.T.A. complimented the principal on the quality of her administration.
4. It is difficult to be critical of such a prominent and dignified American official.
5. The citizens voted for a president who supported security and a sound economy.
6. Abigail has the aptitude for a musical career.
7. Our principal believes that mental activity is no substitute for physical activity.
8. Ability to read is a practical necessity in our society.
9. Please do not hesitate to notify me if there is any significant change in plans.
10. Ms. Edison wrote a sensitive article for the institute's newsletter.
11. In reality, Oliver made an intelligent decision about the medical advice.

Take out a piece of blank paper. Your teacher will dictate three of the sentences above for you to write.

Now select ten words from List 34 and create a short story or a descriptive paragraph that uses those words. Be creative and avoid repetition!

Reading Accuracy: Demonstrate your accuracy in reading and spelling List 34 words. Your teacher will select ten words to read and ten practical spelling words for you to spell. Record your scores on the Accuracy Checklist. Work toward 90–100 percent accuracy.

Reading Proficiency: Now build up your reading fluency with List 34 words. Decide on your rate goal with your teacher. Record your progress on the Proficiency Graph.

My goal for reading List 34 is ________ words per minute with two or fewer errors.

WORKSHEET 35–A

Review: *i* in an unaccented middle syllable usually says /ə/.

In some words, *i* in an unaccented middle syllable says /ē/, and *u* in an unaccented middle syllable says /ə/.

i often says /ē/ when it is part of a middle syllable that precedes a syllable beginning with a vowel. Circle the syllable in which *i* says /ē/ in the following words.

stu di o	ra di ant	o pi um	de vi ate	ma lar i a
so di um	o be di ence	au di ence	ser i ous	ma ter i al
char i ot	su per i or	me di ate	sta di um	pho bi a

u is sometimes found in the middle syllable of a multisyllabic word. The *u* is pronounced differently in various parts of the United States. Dictionaries use the following ways to repιesent the sound: /ə/, /o͞o/, /yə/, /yo͞o/, or /ū/. Circle the syllable with *u* in the following words.

an nu al	man u al	pop u lar	ac tu al	mon u ment
sen su ous	cas u al	vis u al	con tin u ous	doc u ment

Some common endings with unaccented *i* and *u* are listed below. Write each ending three times, saying it aloud as you write it.

-ial says /ē əl/ (radial)	ial	ial	ial
-ious says /ē əs/ (serious)	ious	ious	ious
-iate says /ē āt/ (radiate)	iate	iate	iate
-ual says /ū əl/ (gradual)	ual	ual	ual

Circle and pronounce the endings in the following words.

radial	appreciate	punctual	memorial	various
serious	editorial	continual	congenial	radiate
mediate	previous	furious	annual	usual

WORKSHEET 35–B

Review: *i* often says /ē/ when it is part of a middle syllable that precedes a syllable beginning with a vowel.

Your teacher will dictate some syllables in which unaccented *i* is pronounced /ē/. Say each syllable aloud as you spell it.

1. ni	4. vi	6. tri	8. i
2. di	5. bi	7. mi	9. li
3. ci			10. pi

Review: How do you spell the ending pronounced /ē əl/? ial

How do you spell the ending pronounced /ē əs/? ious

How do you spell the ending pronounced /ē āt/? iate

Circle and write the syllable in which *i* is pronounced /ē/ in the following words. It will be one of the ten syllables that you spelled above.

industrial	tri	portfolio	li
audience	di	phobia	bi
deviate	vi	appreciate	ci
maniac	ni	various	i
opium	pi	premium	mi

Match the word parts to make real words. Then say each word aloud as you write it.

grad	ious	gradual	ra	ual	radio
glor	ial	glorious	man	ular	manual
stu	ual	studio	pop	ious	popular
triv	dio	trivial	cur	dio	curious

WORKSHEET 35–C

In List 35 words, the accent is on the syllable *just before* the unaccented syllable with *i* (/ē/) or *u*.

Circle the middle syllables that contain unaccented *i* (/ē/) or unaccented *u*. Draw a box around the accented syllable. If the vowel in the accented syllable is long or short, mark it. Then pronounce and combine the syllables to read the whole word.

rā di al	radial
or i ole	oriole
pŏp u lar	popular
ma lar i a	malaria
ŏb vi ous	obvious
cen tĕn ni al	centennial
ăn nu al	annual
mŏn u ment	monument
pŭnc tu ate	punctuate
ō pi um	opium
ĕn vi ous	envious
ex pē di ent	expedient

su per i or	superior
stū di o	studio
im mē di ate	immediate
ĭd i ot	idiot
sub ŭr bi a	suburbia
sō di um	sodium
trĭv i al	trivial
stĭm u lant	stimulant
con spĭc u ous	conspicuous
diph ther i a	diphtheria
rā di o	radio
mē di um	medium

Unscramble these multisyllabic words.

gu sin lar	singular	vi ob ous	obvious
i id ot	idiot	um di sta	stadium
u doc ment	document	u lar pop	popular
o di ra	radio	cur ous i	curious
or i per su	superior	di ent o be	obedient
tic lar u par	particular	tri in dus al	industrial

WORKSHEET 35–D

Your teacher will dictate some words. Sound out each word as you write the missing syllable(s). Then write the whole word, saying it aloud as you spell it. Remember: If you hear the long-*e* sound in a middle syllable, it is spelled *i*. The schwa or long-*u* sound in a middle syllable is spelled *u*.

	Copy
1. triv i a	trivia
2. so di um	sodium
3. ra di a tor	radiator
4. su per i or	superior
5. o pi um	opium
6. im me di ate	immediate
7. cus to di an	custodian
8. en vi ous	envious
9. hu mil i ate	humiliate
10. con ge ni al	congenial
11. pop u lar	popular
12. mon u ment	monument
13. con grat u late	congratulate
14. an nu al	annual
15. u su al	usual
16. ri dic u lous	ridiculous

*Write four words from above under each heading.

i Says /ē/		*u* Says /ə/	
trivia	radiator	popular	annual
sodium	superior	monument	usual

* Answers will vary.

WORKSHEET 35–E

-ial (/ē əl/) and *ious* (/ē əs/) are common endings.

Fill in the missing ending to make a word. Then write each word next to its definition.

Add *ious*		
* obvious	1. Extremely angry	furious
envious	2. Eager to learn or know	curious
* previous	3. Doubtful	dubious
* various	4. Spiteful; jealous	envious
* furious	5. Different; diverse	various
* curious	6. Easy to see or understand	obvious
dubious	7. Thoughtful; important; not fooling	serious
* serious	8. Occurring before; prior	previous

Add *ial*		
* material	9. A reminder of a person or event	memorial
colonial	10. Having to do with industry	industrial
* memorial	11. Compatible; getting along well together	congenial
serial	12. Relating to colonies	colonial
centennial	13. Having to do with 100 years	centennial
* industrial	14. Of a series	serial
congenial	15. What something is made from	material
* editorial	16. A newspaper article that gives an opinion	editorial

Have another student test you on spelling the starred words. They are practical spelling words.

My score: ______ words correct.

WORKSHEET 35–F

-iate (/ē āt/) and *-ual* are common endings.

Fill in the missing ending to make a word. Then write each word next to its definition.

Add *iate*		
humiliate	1. To send out rays of heat	radiate
radiate	2. To relieve or lessen	alleviate
* appreciate	3. To try to settle a disagreement	mediate
retaliate	4. To degrade or lower the pride of	humiliate
deviate	5. To pay back or take revenge	retaliate
mediate	6. To turn aside	deviate
* appropriate	7. To think well of; to value	appreciate
alleviate	8. To take for one's own	appropriate

Add *ual*		
* annual	9. Not deliberate; occurring by chance	casual
* visual	10. On time	punctual
factual	11. Reciprocal; shared in common	mutual
* casual	12. Occurring yearly	annual
* usual	13. Having to do with sight or vision	visual
mutual	14. Real; actual; containing facts	factual
* gradual	15. Changing little by little	gradual
* punctual	16. Never stopping	continual
* continual	17. Common; ordinary; in common use	usual

Have another student test you on spelling the starred words. They are practical spelling words.

My score: ________ words correct.

WORKSHEET 35–G

A word family is a group of words that have a common part. Adding various endings to the common part changes the part of speech or alters the meaning. For example, *memory, memorial, memorize,* and *memorandum* are members of the same word family. The common part is *memor,* which means "remember."

For each of the words below, make a member of its word family by adding one of these endings: *-iate, -ial, -ual,* or *-ious.* You may need to drop one or more letters before adding the ending. Use a dictionary if you need help.

anniversary	annual	humility	humiliate
vision	visual	glory	glorious
appreciation	appreciate	memory	memorial
continue	continual	vary	various
fury	furious	trivia	trivial
colony	colonial	editor	editorial
melody	melodious	industry	industrial (ious)
fact	factual	mystery	mysterious
envy	envious	tedium	tedious

Find and circle the eighteen words you wrote above in the puzzle below. The words can be found in a straight line across or up and down.

M E M O R I A L A J T I Y E D I T O R I A L
T E D I O U S B C O L O N I A L R U V J N K
C L V F K F G L O R I O U S Z N I G I L N W
V X M U A A O H N E N V I O U S V N S M U D
A P P R E C I A T E M Y S T E R I O U S A Y
R E N I Z T O B I P Q P I A V S A I A P L A
I B Q O C U J I N D U S T R I A L R L C O F
O G P U D A S H U M I L I A T E D Q K T E Q
U R F S U L E L A V H I N D U S T R I O U S
S I H W F R M E L O D I O U S D X T M X G S

WORKSHEET 35–H

u usually occurs alone in an unaccented syllable *(man u al, ri dic u lous, con tin u ous)*. However, in some words *u* joins the consonant before it to form a new sound.

In unaccented middle syllables with *tu*, *t* says /ch/ *(actual)*.
In unaccented middle syllables with *du*, *d* says /j/ *(graduate)*.

Fill in the blanks with *tu* or *du*.

Add *tu*	Copy	Add *du*	Copy
* ac tu al	actual	e du cate	educate
mu tu al	mutual	sche du ling	scheduling
* punc tu al	punctual	resi du al	residual
* fac tu al	factual	* gra du ate	graduate
si tu ate	situate	e du cation	education
ac tu ate	actuate	gra du ation	graduation
spa tu la	spatula	* gra du al	gradual
mor tu ary	mortuary	e du cator	educator
* punc tu ate	punctuate	indivi du al	individual
taran tu la	tarantula		
* congra tu late	congratulate		
perpe tu al	perpetual		
fluc tu ate	fluctuate		
contemp tu ous	contemptuous		
punc tu ation	punctuation		

Have another student test you on spelling the starred words. They are practical spelling words.

My score: ______ words correct.

WORKSHEET 35–I

Add one of the four endings below to make a word out of each word part. Then write each word under the correct heading.

-iate *-ious* *-ial* *-ual*

mut ual	dev iate
centenn ial	dev ious
fur ious	apprec iate
grad ual	vis ual
humil iate	us ual
obv ious	cur ious
mater ial	immed iate
ser ious	memor ial
ser ial	prev ious
contin ual	industr ious
retal iate	industr ial
rad iate	appropr iate
rad ial	colon ial
punct ual	

-ial	*-iate*	*-ious*	*-ual*
centennial	humiliate	furious	mutual
material	retaliate	obvious	gradual
serial	radiate	serious	continual
radial	deviate	devious	punctual
memorial	appreciate	curious	visual
industrial	immediate	previous	usual
colonial	appropriate	industrious	

WORKSHEET 35–J

In the following words, identify the syllable that contains an unaccented *i* (/ē/) or *u*. Then copy the words by syllables, writing the accented syllables in the boxes. Mark long and short accented vowels and pronounce the words.

Review: The accented syllable comes just before the syllable with unaccented *i* (/ē/) or *u*.

	Accented Syllable	Unaccented Syllable with *i* or *u*			Accented Syllable	Unaccented Syllable with *i* or *u*	
phobia	phō	bi	a	obvious	ŏb	vi	ous
chariot	char	i	ot	manual	măn	u	al
popular	pŏp	u	lar	casual	căs	u	al
premium	prē	mi	um	graduate	grad	u	ate *
studio	stū	di	o	median	mē	di	an
serious	ser	i	ous	monument	mŏn	u	ment

		Accented Syllable	Unaccented Syllable with *i* or *u*	
delirium	de	lir	i	um
colonial	col	ō	ni	al
superior	su	per	i	or
material	ma	ter	i	al
continuous	con	tĭn	u	ous

* Allow credit for gra·du·ate.

WORKSHEET 35–K

By adding suffixes or endings, you can create new members of a word family for many words in List 35. In some cases, the longer words have *two* accented syllables: a primary accent and a secondary accent.

Read the words below and write them by syllables. Notice the accent patterns.*

Three-Syllable Words				Four-Syllable Words				
radiate	ra	di	ate	radiation	ra'	di	a	tion
*graduate	grad	u	ate	graduation	grad'	u	a	tion
punctuate	punc	tu	ate	punctuation	punc'	tu	a	tion
mediate	me	di	ate	mediation	me'	di	a	tion
*educate	ed	u	cate	education	ed'	u	ca	tion
deviate	de	vi	ate	deviation	de'	vi	a	tion
various	var	i	ous	variation	var'	i	a	tion

In the next group, the four-syllable words have only a primary accent.

previous	pre	vi	ous	previously	pre	vi	ous	ly
serious	ser	i	ous	seriously	ser	i	ous	ly
obvious	ob	vi	ous	obviously	ob	vi	ous	ly

A primary accent is on the syllable before -*tion*.

Either a primary or secondary accent is on the syllable before the syllable with unaccented *i* or *u*.

* ☐ = syllable with primary accent
___' = syllable with secondary accent
▒ = syllable with unaccented *i* or *u*

*Allow credit for gra·du·ate and e·du·cate.

WORKSHEET 35–L

Study the word family pairs below. In the left column, circle the syllable with unaccented *i* or *u* and draw a box around the accented syllable. In the right column, write the related word by syllables. Write the syllable with unaccented *i* or *u* in the shaded area and the syllable with the primary accent in the box. Compare the accent patterns.

Remember: In most words, a primary accent comes just before the syllable with unaccented *i* or *u*. If a word ends in *tion* or *ity*, a primary accent comes just before the ending, and a secondary accent comes just before the syllable with unaccented *i* or *u*.

Five-Syllable Words

appreciate	appreciation	ap	pre'	ci	a	tion	
continual	continuation	con	tin'	u	a	tion	
humiliate	humiliation	hu	mil'	i	a	tion	
document	documentation	doc'	u	men	ta	tion	
curious	curiosity	cur'	i	os	i	ty	
continual	continually	con	tin	u	al	ly	
expedient	expediency	ex	pe	di	en	cy	
immediate	immediately	im	me	di	ate	ly	

Six- and Seven-Syllable Words

visualize	visualization	vis'	u	al	i	za	tion	
deteriorate	deterioration	de	ter'	i	or	a	tion	
actual	actualization	ac'	tu	al	i	za	tion	
industrial	industrialization	in	dus'	tri	al	i	za	tion

WORKSHEET 35–M

Add one of the endings below to complete each word part. Then write the whole word, saying it aloud as you write it.

-io = /ē ō/ *-ia* = /ē ə/ *-ium* = /ē əm/ *-iac* = /ē ăk/

tēd ium	tedium	card iac	cardiac
ōp ium	opium	delir ium	delirium
portfōl io	portfolio	diphther ia	diphtheria
rād io (ium)	radio	suburb ia	suburbia
phōb ia	phobia	malar ia	malaria
sōd ium	sodium	auditor ium	auditorium
zōd iac	zodiac	triv ia	trivia
mān ia (iac)	mania	aquar ium	aquarium
stūd io	studio	condomin ium	condominium
mēd ia (ium)	media		
stād ium	stadium		

Now, write three words from above under each heading and practice reading each list to build up your speed.

-ium	*-ia*	*-iac*	*-io*
Answers will vary.			

Proofing Practice: Two common List 35 words are misspelled in each of the sentences below. Correct them as shown.

1. The new curriculum was not ~~populer~~ popular; most of the graduates had not ~~apreciated~~ appreciated it.
2. The audience applauded ~~enthuseastically~~ enthusiastically when the new ~~aquariam~~ aquarium was opened.
3. Tuberculosis, diphtheria, and ~~malarya~~ malaria can be very ~~sereous~~ serious diseases.
4. The oriole is a ~~concpicuus~~ conspicuous bird with its ~~gloreous~~ glorious orange coloring.

WORKSHEET 35–N

Your teacher will dictate some practical spelling words from List 35. Say the words aloud as you write them under the correct heading.

ious	*ial*	*ium*
previous	memorial	stadium
obvious	material	medium
various	industrial	
serious		

iate	*ior*
immediate	superior
appreciate	inferior

ual	*ument*	*ular*
casual	document	particular
visual		popular
continual		singular
usual		
actual		

Find and circle the twenty-two words above in the puzzle below. The words can be found in a straight line across or up and down.

C	O	N	T	I	N	U	A	L	A	V	I	S	U	A	L	M	A	T	E	R	I	A	L	S	B
A	C	P	A	R	T	I	C	U	L	A	R	D	S	I	N	G	U	L	A	R	E	J	O	T	S
S	E	R	I	O	U	S	T	F	K	R	P	S	U	P	E	R	I	O	R	T	W	Z	D	A	N
U	P	R	E	V	I	O	U	S	G	I	L	Q	A	I	M	M	E	D	I	A	T	E	U	D	Y
A	P	P	R	E	C	I	A	T	E	O	H	M	L	R	M	E	M	O	R	I	A	L	V	I	X
L	I	N	P	O	P	U	L	A	R	U	I	N	F	E	R	I	O	R	O	B	V	I	O	U	S
M	E	D	I	U	M	I	N	D	U	S	T	R	I	A	L	D	O	C	U	M	E	N	T	M	O

WORKSHEET 35–O

Many place names end in *ia*. This ending is often pronounced /ē ə/, but sometimes it is pronounced /yə/. Complete these place names by adding *ia*. Say each word aloud as you write it.

Colomb ia	Colombia	Slovak ia	Slovakia
Austr ia	Austria	Saudi Arab ia	Saudi Arabia
Syr ia	Syria	Sardin ia	Sardinia
Bulgar ia	Bulgaria	Ind ia	India
Niger ia	Nigeria	Boliv ia	Bolivia
Pennsylvan ia	Pennsylvania	Philadelph ia	Philadelphia
Mongol ia	Mongolia	Alban ia	Albania
Suman ia	Rumania	Austral ia	Australia

Unscramble the words below to find three place names from the list above in which *ia* is pronounced /yə/.

ARAILATUS A U S T R A L I A

AIMONLOG M O N G O L I A

NANNYSAVELIP P E N N S Y L V A N I A

In other place names, unaccented *i* says /ē/. Add *i* and another vowel to complete these place names.

Eth i o pia	Ethiopia	Ontar i o	Ontario
Louis i a na	Louisiana	Sov i e t Union	Soviet Union

The names of some diseases, illnesses, or mental conditions also end in *ia*. Complete the words below. Then circle the four words in which *ia* says /ē ə/. Put a check in front of the word in which *ia* says /yə/. Put a star in front of the word in which *ia* says /chə/.

(diphther i a)	(phob i a)	(man i a)
(malar i a)	✓ pneumon i a	★ dement i a

WORKSHEET 35–P

Many of the words in List 35 are adjectives (describing words). Fill in each blank with the adjective that makes sense in the sentence.

envious	furious	previous	tedious	ridiculous
obedient	strenuous	manual	obvious	serious
annual	industrial	usual	punctual	glorious

1. After a strenuous hike up the mountain, we rested and enjoyed the glorious view.
2. Juliet's previous marriages ended in divorce, so she was a little nervous about getting married again.
3. On a hot day, Marie is envious of people who have swimming pools.
4. Emmanuel wishes that his dog, Claudius, were more obedient.
5. The answer is so obvious I can't believe that you don't know it.
6. Ms. Zaviar was furious because the children broke her studio window.
7. Getting suspended from school is a serious matter.
8. It was ridiculous for Samuel to think he could hitchhike to Korea.
9. Sophia makes an annual trip to Peoria to buy her fall wardrobe.
10. Indianapolis is a city characterized by industrial development.
11. Manual labor can be tedious and repetitious.
12. As usual, Harriet was late; I have never known her to be punctual.

Unscramble the words below and spell them correctly in the blanks and circles. All the words can be found in the list above.

OUTSIDE T(E)DIOU(S)

OVERISUP PREVI(O)U(S)

TRAINUSLID (I)ND(U)ST(R)IAL

Unscramble the letters you have written in the circles to make another word from the list above:

SERIOUS

WORKSHEET 35–Q

Use the words below to complete the puzzle. Use a dictionary to look up the meaning of unfamiliar words.

delirium	malaria	phobia	monument
trivial	accordian	tedium	conspicuous
diphtheria	premium	median	custodian
expedient	dubious	sodium	deteriorate

Across

4. Something set up to keep alive a memory of a person or event
5. In the middle; intermediate
8. A wild, excited state of mind
9. A musical instrument
11. A prize or reward to encourage one to buy; a bonus
14. An infectious disease
15. Obvious; easily seen
16. Guardian; caretaker of a building

Down

1. A chemical found in salt
2. Make or become worse
3. A disease spread by mosquitos
6. Useful; helping to reach an end
7. Unimportant
10. Uncertain; causing doubt
12. Tiresomeness
13. An irrational fear of something

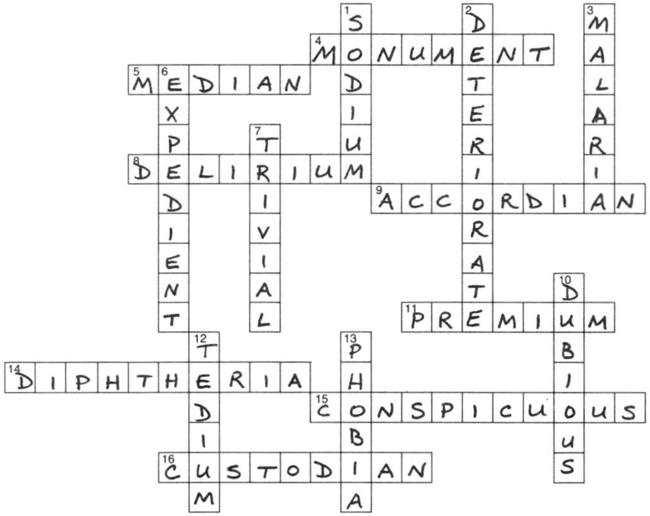

WORKSHEET 35–R

Read the following sentences and circle all the List 35 words that you can find.

1. The custodian had the tedious job of vacuuming the mortuary every evening.
2. The audience in the stadium applauded the champion in the chariot race.
3. The editorial suggests erecting a memorial monument to the Olympic champions.
4. The librarian was furious when he discovered that the documents were fraudulent.
5. The annual graduation ceremony was held in the auditorium.
6. Harriet had to reread the manual to repair the radiator in her studio.
7. The new history curriculum is filled with trivial information; the previous one was more serious.
8. The colonial settlers felt that they were superior and that the native people were barbarians.
9. The oriole has a melodious voice.
10. The young executive had little experience but much enthusiasm.

Take out a piece of blank paper. Your teacher will dictate three of the sentences above for you to write.

Now select ten words from List 35 and create a short story or a descriptive paragraph that uses those words. Be creative and avoid repetition!

Reading Accuracy: Demonstrate your accuracy in reading and spelling List 35 words. Your teacher will select ten words to read and ten practical spelling words for you to spell. Record your scores on the Accuracy Checklist. Work toward 90–100 percent accuracy.

Reading Proficiency: Now build up your reading fluency with List 35 words. Decide on your rate goal with your teacher. Record your progress on the Proficiency Graph.

My goal for reading List 35 is ________ words per minute with two or fewer errors.

WORKSHEET 36–A

i usually says /y/ when it is in an unaccented syllable and is preceded by *l* or *n*. Circle the syllables in which *i* says /y/ in the following words.

mil lion	fa mil iar	con ve nient	o pin ion
pe cu liar	com pan ion	Dan iel	bril liant
on ion	Wil liam	val iant	u nion
le nient	gar de nia	com mu nion	stal lion
I tal ian	Span iard	ju nior	re bel lious

ion says /yən/ at the end of quite a few List 36 words. Circle *ion* in the words below; then copy the words and write them in alphabetical order.

	Copy	ABC Order
billion	billion	billion
stallion	stallion	bunion
bunion	bunion	communion
companion	companion	companion
communion	communion	million
opinion	opinion	onion
rebellion	rebellion	opinion
onion	onion	rebellion
million	million	stallion

In all the words above *i* says /y/. The letter that comes just before *i* is either __l__ or __n__.

Match each group of letters with its sound.

ial — /yəl/
ient — /yənt/
ior — /yer/

iant — /yənt/
ia — /yə/
ian — /yən/

WORKSHEET 36–B

When *i* says /y/ in the last syllable of a word, that syllable is unaccented and often has the schwa sound.

Key: If you hear . . . ,	it is usually spelled . . .
/yən/	*ion* or *ian*
/yə/	*ia*
/yer/	*ior* or *iar*
/yəl/	*ial* or *iel*
/yənt/	*ient* or *iant*

Your teacher will dictate final syllables that contain unaccented *i*. Say the syllable aloud as you spell it. Use the key above.

1. ion or ian
2. ia
3. ial or iel
4. ior or iar
5. iant or ient
6. iel or ial
7. ion or ian
8. ient or iant
9. ia
10. iar or ior

Circle the final syllable in which *i* says /y/ in each of the words below. Then write the final syllable. Each syllable will be the same as one of the syllables you spelled above.

petunia	ia	familiar	iar
senior	ior	lenient	ient
valiant	iant	onion	ion
Daniel	iel	congenial	ial
Virginia	ia	million	ion

WORKSHEET 36–C

When *i* says /y/, it is in an unaccented syllable, usually at the end of a word. The accent is on the syllable *just before* the final syllable.

Circle the syllable in which *i* says /y/. Draw a box around the accented syllable and mark the accented vowel. Then pronounce and combine the syllables to read the whole word.

com păn ion	companion
o pĭn ion	opinion
re bĕl lion	rebellion
mag nō ia	magnolia
fa mĭl iar	familiar
pe cū liar	peculiar
con gē nial	congenial
pe tū nia	petunia
par a pher nā ia	paraphernalia

Vir gĭn ia	Virginia
gar dē nia	gardenia
me dăl lion	medallion
do mĭn ion	dominion
I tăl ian	Italian
ci vĭl ian	civilian
be gō nia	begonia
Bra zĭl ian	Brazilian

Match the syllables to make real words. Say each word aloud as you write it.

mil	ion	million	ge	ion	genius
se	nior	senior	val	nius	valiant
Wil	lion	William	on	iel	onion
bun	liam	bunion	Dan	iant	Daniel

Review: In the words above, the unaccented *i* says /y/.

The syllable in which *i* says /y/ is unaccented (accented, unaccented).

The accent is on the syllable just before the final syllable.

WORKSHEET 36–D

Your teacher will dictate some words. Sound out each word as you write the missing syllable(s). Then write the whole word, saying it aloud as you spell it.

Since the endings are unaccented and have the schwa sound, it may be difficult to tell which vowel to use. To help you, the words are grouped by common endings.

Remember: The /y/ sound is spelled by *i* preceded by *l* or *n*.

	Copy	ABC Order
1. bun ion	bunion	Brazilian
2. com pan ion	companion	bunion
3. o pin ion	opinion	civilian
4. do min ion	dominion	companion
5. se nior	senior	convenient
6. ju nior	junior	dominion
7. le nient	lenient	inconvenient
8. in con ve nient	inconvenient	Italian
9. con ve nient	convenient	junior
10. Vir gin ia	Virginia	lenient
11. pe tu nia	petunia	magnolia
12. mag nol ia	magnolia	opinion
13. ci vil ian	civilian	petunia
14. I tal ian	Italian	senior
15. Bra zil ian	Brazilian	Virginia

The five endings in which *i* says /y/ above are ion, ior, ient, ia, and ian.

Now go back and write the words in alphabetical order.

WORKSHEET 36–E

Match the syllables to make real words. Say each word aloud as you write it.

Syllables	Word	Syllables	Word
mil — lior / lion / liar	million	āl — ia / iar / ien	alien
val — iant / ion / ia	valiant	Wil — lia / lion / liam	William

Unscramble these three-syllable words.

mil iar fa	familiar	nial con ge	congenial
ion pan com	companion	pin ion o	opinion
bel lion re	rebellion	ia gin Vir	Virginia

Complete the words by adding one of the endings. Then write the whole word.

-ion or *-ior*		*-ian* or *-iar*	
compan ion	companion	famil iar	familiar
jun ior	junior	civil ian	civilian
mill ion	million	pecul iar	peculiar
opin ion	opinion	Ital ian	Italian
sen ior	senior	Brazil ian	Brazilian

-iel or *-ient*		*-ia* or *-iant*	
span iel	spaniel	begon ia	begonia
len ient	lenient	brill iant	brilliant
conven ient	convenient	petun ia	petunia
Dan iel	Daniel	val iant	valiant

WORKSHEET 36–F

Write the words under the correct heading.

onion	civilian	opinion	senior	familiar
junior	begonia	valiant	petunia	medallion
congenial	Daniel	spaniel	convenient	peculiar
bunion	Virginia	magnolia	companion	brilliant

ion or *ian* = /yən/	*ior* or *iar* = /yər/	*ia* = /yə/
onion	junior	begonia
bunion	senior	Virginia
civilian	familiar	magnolia
opinion	peculiar	petunia
companion		
medallion		

iant or *ient* = /yənt/	*ial* or *iel* = /yəl/
valiant	congenial
convenient	Daniel
brilliant	spaniel

Find and circle the twenty words above in the puzzle below. The words can be found in a straight line across or up and down.

A	C	O	N	V	E	N	I	E	N	T	N	T	A	G	M	S	R	W	T	B	S	B	U	N	I	O	N
C	P	P	D	A	B	E	G	O	N	I	A	C	O	N	G	E	N	I	A	L	P	E	T	U	N	I	A
B	R	I	L	L	I	A	N	T	E	C	I	O	N	D	A	N	I	E	L	Q	A	C	U	E	K	Y	F
G	E	N	C	I	V	I	L	I	A	N	K	V	I	R	G	I	N	I	A	S	N	U	F	R	D	N	H
I	X	I	F	A	M	I	L	I	A	R	E	J	O	Z	C	O	M	P	A	N	I	O	N	W	B	R	L
M	P	O	X	N	J	U	N	I	O	R	Y	A	N	D	N	R	J	F	Z	P	E	C	U	L	I	A	R
L	S	N	H	T	D	M	E	D	A	L	L	I	O	N	Q	M	A	G	N	O	L	I	A	V	O	B	K

WORKSHEET 36–G

Write the following words by syllables according to their accent patterns. Write the accented syllables in the boxes.

William	familiar	brilliant	opinion
million	Daniel	peculiar	rebellious

[Wil]	liam	fa	[mil]	iar
[mil]	lion	pe	[cu]	liar
[Dan]	iel	o	[pin]	ion
[bril]	liant	re	[bel]	lious

Use the words above to complete the following sentences and crossword puzzle.

1. Bill is a nickname for William (5 Across), and Dan is a nickname for Daniel (4 Down).
2. The dictator's opinion (1 Across) was that the rebellious (6 Across) tribes should be defeated.
3. I must know you from somewhere; you look familiar (3 Down).
4. Don't you find it peculiar (2 Down) that our new neighbors never open their drapes?

	1 O	2 P	I	N	I	O	N				
		E									
		C						3 F			
		U			4 D			A			
5 W	I	L	L	I	A	M		M			
		I			N			I			
		A			I			L			
		6 R	E	B	E	L	L	I	O	U	S
					L			A			
								R			

WORKSHEET 36–H

Review: When *i* is in an unaccented syllable and is followed by a vowel, it usually says /ē/. However, *i* says /y/ if it follows *l* or *n*.

Look at each pair of words. In one word *i* says /ē/ and in the other *i* says /y/. Read the words. If the first sound you use for *i* doesn't work, try the other. Circle the *i*; then write the words in the correct column.

radiant	rebellious	phobia
brilliant	furious	magnolia
inferior	experience	congenial
senior	convenience	material
civilian	obedient	superior
librarian	lenient	junior

i Says /ē/	*i* Says /y/
radiant	brilliant
inferior	senior
librarian	civilian
furious	rebellious
experience	convenience
obedient	lenient
phobia	magnolia
material	congenial
superior	junior

Review: After the letters __l__ and __n__, *i* often says /y/.

WORKSHEET 36–I

Your teacher will dictate some practical spelling words from List 36. Say the words aloud as you write them under the correct heading.

Remember: The schwa sound can be spelled several ways. If one way does not look right, try another.

ion	*ian*
onion	Italian
opinion	
million	
union	
companion	

ior	*iar*
junior	peculiar
senior	familiar

ient	*iant*
convenient	brilliant

Proofing Practice: Two List 36 words are misspelled in each of the sentences below. Correct them as shown.

1. The ~~millian~~ million members in the striking auto workers' union were ~~reboleoue~~ rebellious.
2. It was ~~inconveenent~~ inconvenient for my ~~companyun~~ companion to attend the meeting.
3. The ~~seenyor~~ senior class president performed a ~~brillyunt~~ brilliant trumpet solo.
4. The Viking warrior wore a gold ~~medalyon~~ medallion as a sign of his ~~valient~~ valiant deeds.
5. William was ~~famillior~~ familiar with the ~~stalyon's~~ stallion's peculiar behavior.
6. In my ~~opinyon~~ opinion, the ~~junyors~~ juniors should use gardenias for the seniors' graduation flowers.

WORKSHEET 36–J

Add the correct ending to the words below.

-ion	-ior	-ia	-iel
-iant	-iar	-ial	-ient

1. A water dog — span*iel*
2. Odd; different — * pecul*iar*
3. Opposite of junior — * sen*ior*
4. A flowering tree — magnol*ia*
5. A swelling of the big toe — bun*ion*
6. Opposite of strict — len*ient*
7. Well-known — * famil*iar*
8. Handy; suitable; saving trouble — conven*ient*
9. 1,000,000 — * mill*ion*
10. Opposite of senior — * jun*ior*
11. A person who accompanies another — * compan*ion*
12. What one thinks; judgment — * opin*ion*
13. A southern state — Virgin*ia*
14. A vegetable with a bulb-shaped root — * on*ion*
15. An adult male horse — stall*ion*

Have another student test you on spelling the starred words. They are practical spelling words.

My score: ________ words correct.

Review: 1. Two ways to spell the final syllable /yənt/ are *ient* and *iant*.
2. Two ways to spell the final syllable /yər/ are *ior* and *iar*.
3. Two ways to spell the final syllable /yəl/ are *ial* and *iel*.
4. Two ways to spell the final syllable /yən/ are *ion* and *ian*.

WORKSHEET 36–K

Fill in each blank with a word from below that makes sense in the sentence.

dahlias	gardenia	valiant	petunias	lenient
magnolia	bunion	begonias	civilian	inconvenient
genius	medallion		ingenious	congenial

1. Mr. Collier went to the doctor to have a *bunion* removed from his foot.
2. The m*agnolia* tree has large white or pink blossoms.
3. The g*ardenia* is a fragrant flower frequently used in corsages.
4. William Daniels has a garden full of *dahlias*, *begonias*, and *petunias*.
5. After twenty years of military service, Mr. Williams did not know how to keep busy in *civilian* life.
6. He wore a large gold *medallion* around his neck.
7. Whoever invented video games was a real *genius*.
8. Theresa is the most *congenial* person I know; we get along well.
9. Because his parents are too *lenient*, Daniel often misbehaves.
10. Could you call back later; this is an *inconvenient* time for me to talk.
11. The Spaniard proved to be a *valiant* soldier.
12. The *ingenious* girl made a radio set for herself.

Unscramble the words below and spell them correctly in the blanks and circles. Both the words can be found in the list above.

ALLNODIME (M) E D (A) L (L) (I) O N

LAGINCONE C (O) N (G) E (N) I (A) L

Unscramble the letters you have written in the circles to make another word from the list above:

M A G N O L I A

WORKSHEET 36–L

Read the following sentences and circle all the List 36 words that you can find.

1. A labor union led the rebellion against the Brazilian dictator.
2. The soldiers in the tenth batallion were awarded medallions for their valiant deeds.
3. The Australian soccer players put up a brilliant defense against the Italians.
4. Mountain climbing is an inconvenient sport because it requires so much paraphernalia.
5. Nathaniel's cocker spaniel found ingenious ways to escape from the yard.
6. Daniel Williams and his companion Junior Collier won the billiards tournament.
7. Italian Stallion is a peculiar name for a race horse.
8. It seemed as though the Woman's Auxiliary had knit millions, or even billions, of socks and hats for the soldiers.
9. Virginia saw a lot of familiar faces at her tenth reunion.
10. The Aztec civilians were unable to escape the dominion of the Spaniards.

Take out a piece of blank paper. Your teacher will dictate three of the sentences above for you to write.

Now select ten words from List 36 and create a short story or a descriptive paragraph that uses those words. Be creative and avoid repetition!

Reading Accuracy: Demonstrate your accuracy in reading and spelling List 36 words. Your teacher will select ten words to read and ten practical spelling words for you to spell. Record your scores on the Accuracy Checklist. Work toward 90–100 percent accuracy.

Reading Proficiency: Now build up your reading fluency with List 36 words. Decide on your rate goal with your teacher. Record your progress on the Proficiency Graph.

My goal for reading List 36 is ________ words per minute with two or fewer errors.

WORKSHEET 37–A

In some words the letter combinations *ti* and *ci* say /sh/. These letter combinations are attached to other letters to form a single syllable.

Circle the letter combination *ti* or *ci* in each ending below.

-tial	-tious	-tient	-tience
-cial	-cious	-cient	-cience

List the four groups of letters that *ti* and *ci* are attached to.

al ous ent ence

Draw a line between each group of letters and its sound.

al	/əs/
ous	/əl/
ent	/əns/
ence	/ənt/

Study and pronounce these endings.

ti says /sh/	*ci* says /sh/
-tial	-cial
-tious	-cious
-tient	-cient
-tience	-cience

Circle and pronounce the final syllable in each word below.

gracious	proficient	financial	patience	ancient
judicious	potential	suspicious	official	artificial
quotient	atrocious	ambitious	provincial	nuptial
cautious	efficient	conscience	confidential	fictitious

WORKSHEET 37–B

Review: *ti* and *ci* say /sh/.

Match each ending with its pronunciation. Each pronunciation will have two endings connected to it.

-tial	/shənt/	-cience
-tious	/shəl/	-cient
-tient	/shəns/	-cious
-tience	/shəs/	-cial

Pronounce these endings in which *ti* and *ci* say /sh/. Then have your teacher or a classmate time you to see how long it takes you to read the list. See if you can improve your time with practice.

-cious	-tial	-tient	-cience	-cial
-tience	-cient	-tious	-cial	-tion
-tial	-tience	-cious	-cian	-tious
-cial	-tial	-cience	-tious	-tient
-cient	-tience	-cious	-tion	-cian

Trial 1: ______ seconds Trial 2: ______ seconds Trial 3: ______ seconds

List two ways to spell the ending that says /shəl/. tial cial

List two ways to spell the ending that says /shəs/. tious cious

List two ways to spell the ending that says /shənt/. tient cient

List two ways to spell the ending that says /shəns/. tience cience

Review: List three ways to spell the ending that says /shən/. tion sion cian

Circle the endings that begin with *ti* or *ci*. Match each ending with its pronunciation.

patience	/shəs/	delicious
ambitious	/shəns/	conscience

WORKSHEET 37–C

Always accent the syllable *just before* a final syllable that begins with *ti* or *ci*. The accented syllable has a clear vowel sound according to its syllabic type (short, long, *r*-controlled, or double vowel).

Circle the endings that begin with *ti* or *ci*. Draw a box around the accented syllable. If the vowel in the accented syllable is long or short, mark it. Then pronounce and combine the syllables to read the whole word.

sō cial	social
pā tience	patience
spē cious	specious
quō tient	quotient
nŭp tial	nuptial
cŏn science	conscience

in fĕc tious	infectious
ten ā cious	tenacious
cre dĕn tial	credential
flir tā tious	flirtatious
im par tial	impartial
pre cŏ cious	precocious

If the accented syllable that comes just before a *ti* or *ci* syllable ends with the letter *i*, give the *i* an accented *short* sound, /ĭ/.

in ĭ tial	initial
sus pĭ cious	suspicious
fic tĭ tious	fictitious
suf fĭ cient	sufficient
ar ti fĭ cial	artificial

aus pĭ cious	auspicious
ju dĭ cial	judicial
nu trĭ tious	nutritious
vĭ cious	vicious
su per stĭ tious	superstitious

Match the word parts to make real words. Then say the words as you write them.

finan	tial	financial
poten	cious	potential
deli	cial	delicious

cau	tial	cautious
pa	tious	patient
essen	tient	essential

WORKSHEET 37–D

In most two- and three-syllable words, the accent is on the first syllable. However, when a *ti* or *ci* syllable is added to the end of a word, the accent pattern changes. The accent is always on the syllable *just before* a final syllable that begins with *ti* or *ci*.

In each word below, draw a box around the accented syllable and mark the accented vowel. Then pronounce and combine the syllables to read the whole word. Remember to give the vowel in the accented syllable a clear vowel sound according to its syllabic type. Remember that *i* before *ti* or *ci* is always short (/ĭ/).

[fī] nance	fi [năn] cial
[ĕs] sence	es [sĕn] tial
[bĕn] e fit	ben e [fĭ] cial
[măl] ice	ma [lĭ] cious
[cŏn] fi dent	con fi [dĕn] tial
[ŏf] fice	of [fĭ] cial
[cŏm] merce	com [mer] cial
[prĕs] i dent	pres i [dĕn] tial
[pō] tent	po [tĕn] tial
[sē] quence	se [quĕn] tial
[rĕs] i dent	res i [dĕn] tial
[sŭb] stance	sub [stăn] tial
[fĭc] tion	fic [tĭ] tious

In the following words, *e* before the *ci* syllable is short, /ĕ/, rather than long. Remember these common exceptions.

[spĕ] cial   es [pĕ] cial ly   [prĕ] cious

Review: Accent the first syllable in most two- and three-syllable words.

When you add a *ti* or *ci* syllable to the end of a word, the accent pattern changes.

WORKSHEET 37–E

Review: The accent always falls on the syllable just before a final syllable that begins with *ti* or *ci*.

i before a *ti* or *ci* ending has a short sound.

Match the syllables to make real words. Say each word aloud as you write it.

pa	cial	patience	prĕ	cial	precious
so	tient	social	spĕ	cious	special
vĭ	tience	vicious	cru	cious	crucial
quo	cious	quotient	lus	cial	luscious

Unscramble these multisyllabic words.

fi con tial den	confidential
cious li de	delicious
pi cious sus	suspicious
ly pe es cial	especially
suf cient fi	sufficient
per su sti tious	superstitious
ar cial fi ti	artificial
tious fec in	infectious

Fill in the blanks with *tial, tious, tient,* or *tience* to complete the words.

You must have patience to find the quotient in long division.

The ambitious candidate entered the presidential election.

I was asked to keep this information confidential.

Chicken pox is an infectious disease.

Are you superstitious about walking under ladders?

WORKSHEET 37–F

cious or *tious*?

The /shəs/ sound is usually spelled *cious*. Fill in the missing syllable, *cious*, and then write the word next to its definition.

* cons<u>cious</u>	1. Very pleasing to taste	delicious
* pre<u>cious</u>	2. Pleasant; full of grace	gracious
* uncons<u>cious</u>	3. Wise; having good judgment	judicious
spa<u>cious</u>	4. Aware; able to feel	conscious
gra<u>cious</u>	5. Unaware; not intended	unconscious
suspi<u>cious</u>	6. Wishing to hurt others	malicious
* deli<u>cious</u>	7. Valuable	precious
judi<u>cious</u>	8. Containing much space	spacious
mali<u>cious</u>	9. Causing one to suspect	suspicious
fero<u>cious</u>	10. Fierce	ferocious

To change a noun that ends in *tion* to an adjective, use *tious* to spell the /shəs/ sound. Change the following *tion* nouns to *tious* adjectives. Then write the adjectives in alphabetical order.

tion Noun		*tious* Adjective	ABC Order
infection	→	infectious	ambitious
caution	→*	cautious	cautious
nutrition	→*	nutritious	flirtatious
superstition	→	superstitious	infectious
flirtation	→	flirtatious	nutritious
ambition	→*	ambitious	superstitious

Have another student test you on spelling the starred words. They are practical spelling words.

My score: ________ words correct.

WORKSHEET 37–G

The /shənt/ sound is usually spelled *cient*. Fill in the missing syllable, *cient*, and copy the whole word.

an<u>cient</u>	ancient	suffi<u>cient</u>	sufficient
omnis<u>cient</u>	omniscient	defi<u>cient</u>	deficient
profi<u>cient</u>	proficient	effi<u>cient</u>	efficient

Learn these two common exceptions. Fill in the blanks with *tient*, and copy the whole word.

pa<u>tient</u> patient quo<u>tient</u> quotient

Complete the puzzle, using the words above.

Across

3. Capable; doesn't waste time
5. Incomplete; defective
6. Knowing everything
7. Enduring calmly
8. Very old

Down

1. Skilled; expert
2. Enough
4. The answer to a division problem

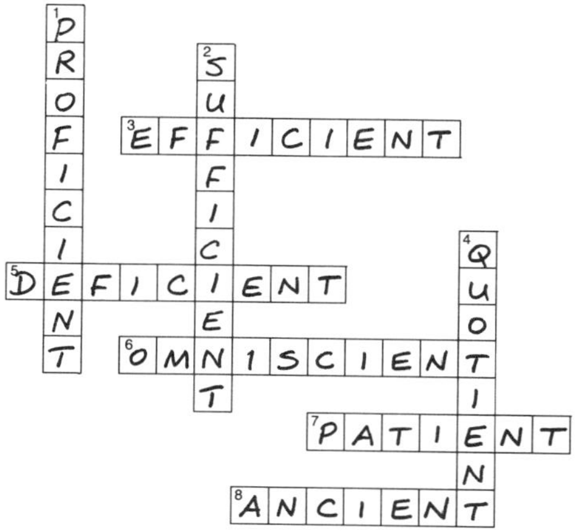

WORKSHEET 37–H

Review: /shəs/ is usually spelled *cious*. Use *tious* if the noun form of the word ends in *tion*.

/shənt/ is usually spelled *cient*. Write the two common exceptions that end in *tient*:

patient and quotient.

Your teacher will dictate some words. Sound out each word as you write the missing syllable(s). Then write the whole word, saying it aloud as you spell it.

	Copy	ABC Order
1. fa cial	facial	ambitious
2. spa cious	spacious	ancient
3. spe cial	special	artificial
4. pa tient	patient	delicious
5. in i tial	initial	especially
6. an cient	ancient	facial
7. un cons cious	unconscious	financial
8. fi nan cial	financial	initial
9. sub stan tial	substantial	nutritious
10. nu tri tious	nutritious	patient
11. ar ti fi cial	artificial	sequential
12. am bi tious	ambitious	spacious
13. se quen tial	sequential	special
14. es pe cial ly	especially	substantial
15. de li cious	delicious	superstitious
16. su per sti tious	superstitious	unconscious

Now go back and write the words in alphabetical order.

WORKSHEET 37–I

In the following words, identify the accented syllable. Then copy the words by syllables under the correct heading, writing the accented syllables in the boxes. Mark long and short accented vowels and pronounce the words.

crucial		[crū]	cial
specious		[spē]	cious
vicious		[vĭ]	cious
ancient		[ān]	cient
nuptial		[nŭp]	tial
patient		[pā]	tient
social		[sō]	cial
commercial	com	[mer]	cial
ambitious	am	[bĭ]	tious
proficient	pro	[fĭ]	cient
sufficient	suf	[fĭ]	cient
ferocious	fe	[rō]	cious
tenacious	ten	[ā]	cious
initial	in	[ĭ]	tial

residential	res	i	[dĕn]	tial
superstitious	su	per	[stĭ]	tious
beneficial	ben	e	[fĭ]	cial
confidential	con	fi	[dĕn]	tial

If an accented syllable ends in a vowel, it usually has a long sound. However, the vowel *i* before a *ti* or *ci* ending has a short sound. Write seven words from above that are examples of this rule.

vicious, ambitious, proficient, sufficient, initial, superstitious, beneficial

WORKSHEET 37–J

Identify the accented syllable in each of the following words. Then copy the words by syllables under the correct heading, writing the accented syllables in the boxes. Mark long and short accented vowels and pronounce the words.

vicious	gracious	confidential	flirtatious	auspicious
residential	financial	patient	beneficial	presidential
judicial	omniscient	artificial	fallacious	partial

Accent the First Syllable

vĭ	cious
grā	cious
pā	tient
par	tial

Accent the Second Syllable

ju	dĭ	cial
fi	năn	cial
om	nĭs	cient
flir	tā	tious
fal	lā	cious
aus	pĭ	cious

Accent the Third Syllable

res	i	dĕn	tial
con	fi	dĕn	tial
ar	ti	fĭ	cial
ben	e	fĭ	cial
pres	i	dĕn	tial

Review: The accent is always on the syllable just before a final syllable that begins with *ti* or *ci*.

WORKSHEET 37–K

-tial and *-cial* are adjective endings. Thinking of a related word can help you decide which ending to use.

face ⟶ facial
impart ⟶ impartial

Underline the final *c* or *t* in the following words. Then write the adjective, which ends in *cial* or *tial*. You may have to drop or change some letters before adding *ial*.

race	racial	part	partial
potent	potential	confident	confidential
justice	judicial	glacier	glacial
office	official	finance	financial
commerce	commercial	president	presidential
province	provincial	resident	residential

There are a few exceptions. Look at them carefully and copy the words.

substance ⟶ substantial — substantial
sequence ⟶ sequential — sequential
essence ⟶ essential — essential
benefit ⟶ beneficial — beneficial
space ⟶ spatial — spatial

Proofing Practice: Two common List 37 words are misspelled in each of the sentences below. Correct them as shown.

1. The museum displayed many ~~preshus~~ precious artifacts from the ~~anchent~~ ancient Greek and Roman civilizations.
2. The ~~delichus~~ delicious meal was very ~~nutrichus~~ nutritious and had no artificial preservatives.
3. It is especially important that you be ~~cauchus~~ cautious in your ~~financhal~~ financial affairs.

WORKSHEET 37–L

Your teacher will dictate some practical spelling words. Say the words aloud as you write them under the correct heading.

	ci Words		*ti* Words
cial	social	*tial*	essential
	special		presidential
	especially		residential
	racial		
	official		
	judicial		
	financial		
cious	conscious	*tious*	cautious
	precious		ambitious
	delicious		nutritious
cient	ancient	*tient*	patient
	efficient		quotient

Find and circle the twenty words above in the puzzle below. The words can be found in a straight line across or up and down.

P	R	E	S	I	D	E	N	T	I	A	L	E	S	P	E	C	I	A	L	L	Y	J
R	E	S	I	D	E	N	T	I	A	L	T	A	P	R	E	S	I	M	E	N	D	U
E	E	S	I	A	L	F	T	W	P	A	T	I	E	N	T	A	M	B	I	T	I	D
C	W	E	F	F	I	C	I	E	N	T	S	O	C	I	A	L	J	I	O	U	S	I
I	D	N	A	N	C	I	E	N	T	O	F	F	I	C	I	A	L	T	I	A	L	C
O	M	T	R	F	I	N	A	N	C	I	A	L	A	C	A	U	T	I	O	U	S	I
U	A	I	B	C	O	N	S	C	I	O	U	S	L	N	Y	Q	U	O	T	I	E	A
S	W	A	O	Q	U	O	T	I	E	N	T	R	A	C	I	A	L	U	W	F	C	L
C	A	L	R	E	S	I	D	E	N	U	T	R	I	T	I	O	U	S	O	C	I	A

WORKSHEET 37–M

Fill in each blank with a word from below that makes sense in the sentence. Use a dictionary to look up unfamiliar words. Underline the phrase in each sentence that gives you a clue to the meaning of the following words.

auspicious	audacious	tenacious	nuptial	fallacious
specious	precocious		martial	omniscient

1. The precocious child learned how to read at the age of three. Her early development was unusual.
2. In most religions, people view their God as omniscient. God has knowledge of everything.
3. The politician convinced us at first that his ideas were sound because he based them on arguments that seemed to be true. We soon discovered, however, that he presented only specious arguments.
4. The store clerk persisted in trying to sell us a model different from the one we wanted. She was a most tenacious salesperson.
5. Don't be misled by the director's unfounded logic. It is fallacious reasoning to base a general rule on just two instances.
6. The nuptial ceremony was held outside in the park. I'm so glad we had good weather for the wedding.
7. My new job looks very promising. Impressing the president of the company was an auspicious beginning.
8. The audacious young man went to the party even though he wasn't invited. It was an overly bold thing to do.
9. The government declared martial law after the uprising. All citizens had to obey the army troops.

Don't be confused by the two words below. Fill in each blank with the correct word.

patients patience

10. It takes a great deal of patience to complete a handmade quilt.
11. The doctor saw several patients at the hospital.

WORKSHEET 37–N

The following groups of words have similar meanings. Read the sentences opposite each group of words and decide which word *best* fits each sentence. Use a dictionary.

luscious
delicious

1. The luscious melon was from Florida.
2. We had a delicious meal at the new restaurant.

judicious
judicial

3. The judicial branch of government enforces the laws of our country.
4. Mario made a judicious decision to go back to school.

efficient
proficient

5. Ms. Fitzgerald doesn't waste any time on the job. She is a(n) efficient administrator.
6. Garrett is a(n) proficient musician.

malicious
vicious
atrocious
ferocious

7. Her eating problem is a(n) vicious cycle; the more she eats, the fatter she gets. The fatter she gets, the more she eats.
8. Nothing can be gained by malicious gossip.
9. The ferocious dog bit its owner on the leg.
10. The criminal committed a(n) atrocious crime.

beneficial
auspicious

11. It is not a(n) auspicious sign that the tree we pruned last fall is bare this spring.
12. This dry climate is beneficial for people who suffer from asthma.

Don't be confused by the two words below. Fill in each blank with the correct word.

conscious
conscience

15. My conscience warned me against doing the wrong thing.
16. He was conscious of a sharp pain in his leg.

WORKSHEET 37–O

Read the following sentences and circle all the List 37 words that you can find.

1. The ambitious young lawyer was especially proficient at handling criminal cases.
2. The nutritious meal was also delicious.
3. The unconscious patient was suffering from an infectious disease.
4. The official financial report suggests great potential for the company.
5. There is an equal racial balance in this residential section of town.
6. In good conscience I cannot support a cut in social security benefits.
7. Mr. Bogart felt anxious about the deficient presidential report he had prepared.
8. The efficient accountant requested a substantial raise in pay.
9. Please give special consideration to this confidential matter.
10. Rebecca was self-conscious during the initial session of the martial arts class.
11. Be cautious with your money around that suspicious looking man.

Take out a piece of blank paper. Your teacher will dictate three of the sentences above for you to write.

Now select ten words from List 37 and create a short story or a descriptive paragraph that uses those words. Be creative and avoid repetition!

Reading Accuracy: Demonstrate your accuracy in reading and spelling List 37 words. Your teacher will select ten words to read and ten practical spelling words for you to spell. Record your scores on the Accuracy Checklist. Work toward 90–100 percent accuracy.

Reading Proficiency: Now build up your reading fluency with List 37 words. Decide on your rate goal with your teacher. Record your progress on the Proficiency Graph.

My goal for reading List 37 is ________ words per minute with two or fewer errors.

WORKSHEET 38–A

Vowel/Vowel combinations (V/V)—Some words with two vowels together divide between the vowels. The first vowel ends a syllable and has a long sound. The second vowel starts the next syllable and may have a long, short, *r*-controlled, or schwa sound.

Practice reading these V/V combinations that are parts of words. Draw a line between the vowels and mark the first vowel long.

eum	pio	eous	vio	oa
iance	uet	ial	ear	oet
ia	uence	dia	rein	riot
uid	coop	eal	uate	eate

Your teacher will dictate some V/V combinations that are parts of words. Say the syllables aloud as you write them. Use the line to divide the syllables.

1. te/or
2. i/o
3. u/al
4. i/um
5. i/ence
6. e/o
7. di/a
8. i/al
9. u/ence
10. co/ag

Underline the V/V combinations in the words below. Draw a line between the vowels and mark the first vowel long. Then write the two vowels.

	V/V		V/V
denial	i / a	zoology	o/o
variety	i / e	theater	e / a
triumphant	i / u	hideous	e / o
annual	u / a	diary	i / a
oasis	o / a	cereal	e / a
poetry	o / e	reunion	e / u
museum	e / u	linear	e / a
theory	e / o	meteor	e / o
fluid	u / i	diamond	i / a

WORKSHEET 38–B

Pronounce and combine the syllables. Then cover the divided word and practice reading the whole word. Study the accent pattern and draw a box around the accented syllable. Underline the V/V combination in the whole word.

—′ —

[tri] al	trial
[cha] os	chaos
[sci] ence	science

— —′ —

re [li] ance	reliance
de [ni] al	denial
tri [um] phant	triumphant

— —′ — —

con [tin] u um	continuum
co [op] er ate	cooperate
zo [ol] o gy	zoology
ge [og] ra phy	geography

— — —′ —

al tru [is] tic	altruistic
in flu [en] tial	influential

— — — —′ —

co or di [na] tion	coordination
co ag u [la] tion	coagulation
co op er [a] tion	cooperation

—′ — —

[cam] e o	cameo
[di] a gram	diagram
[hid] e ous	hideous
[the] a ter	theater

WORKSHEET 38–C

Your teacher will dictate some words. Sound out each word as you write the missing syllable(s). Then write the whole word, saying it aloud as you spell it.

	Copy	ABC Order
1. tri al	trial	altruistic
2. flu id	fluid	cereal
3. di a gram	diagram	cooperation
4. i de al	ideal	diagram
5. vi o let	violet	fluid
6. i o dine	iodine	graduate
7. re ac tion	reaction	ideal
8. cer e al	cereal	influential
9. re li ance	reliance	iodine
10. zo ol o gy	zoology	poetry
11. co op er a tion	cooperation	reaction
12. in flu en tial	influential	reinforce
13. grad u ate	graduate	reliance
14. re in force	reinforce	trial
15. po e try	poetry	violet
16. al tru is tic	altruistic	zoology

Now go back and write the words in alphabetical order.

Review: In Vowel/Vowel combinations, divide between the vowels.

The first vowel ends a syllable and has a long sound.

The second vowel starts the next syllable.

WORKSHEET 38–D

Many words with V/V combinations have a schwa sound in the unaccented syllable. This makes them difficult to spell since it is hard to know which vowel to use. It will be helpful if you recall the spelling of common word endings such as the ones in the headings below.

Say the words aloud as you write them under the correct heading.

* ideal	riotous	* science	influence	triumphant
continuous	reliance	* violence	defiant	* fluent
* cereal	* trial	* annual	* violent	* client

-al = /əl/	*-ant* = /ənt/	*-ence* = /əns/
ideal	defiant	science
cereal	triumphant	violence
trial		influence
annual		

-ance = /əns/	*-ous* = /əs/	*-ent* = /ənt/
reliance	continuous	violent
	riotous	fluent
		client

Don't be confused by the two words below. Fill in each blank with the correct word. Use a dictionary as an aid.

duel
dual

1. The retailer had a dual purpose in selling her merchandise at a 40% discount; one was to attract new customers and the other was to get rid of her summer inventory.
2. During the Middle Ages, it was common for two men to settle their disputes by fighting a duel.

Have another student test you on spelling the starred words. They are practical spelling words.

My score: ________ words correct.

WORKSHEET 38–E

Each of the following words has a syllable with the schwa sound. Identify the vowel that makes the schwa sound, and write each word under the correct heading.

V/V

___	___ ′	ə	___
pri	or	i	ty
ge	om	e	try
an	xi	e	ty
re	al	i	ty
zo	ol	o	gy
	po	e	try
	di	a	gram
	vi	o	lence
	pi	e	ty
	di	a	lect
	the	a	ter
	the	o	ry
	re	a	lize
	vi	o	let
	bo	a	

/ə/ Spelled *a*

diagram
dialect
theater
realize
boa

/ə/ Spelled *e*

geometry
anxiety
poetry
piety

/ə/ Spelled *o*

zoology
violence
theory
violet

/ə/ Spelled *i*

priority
reality

WORKSHEET 38–F

Fill in the missing vowel in each of the practical spelling words below. Then write each word next to its definition and complete the puzzle.

v_i_olent	1. Yearly	annual (7 Down)
ster_e_o	2. Work jointly	cooperate (6 Across)
grad_u_ate	3. One who receives an academic degree	graduate (8 Across)
c_o_operate	4. A building for exhibiting art or historical objects	museum (1 Down)
ann_u_al	5. That which is real	reality (4 Down)
sc_i_ence	6. Systematized knowledge	science (5 Down)
vid_e_o	7. Three-dimensional sound	stereo (5 Across)
mus_e_um	8. A building for watching movies or plays	theater (3 Down)
th_e_ater	9. Used in television	video (2 Down)
r_e_ality	10. Using extreme physical force	violent (2 Across)

Have another student test you on spelling the ten practical spelling words listed above.

My score: ________ words correct.

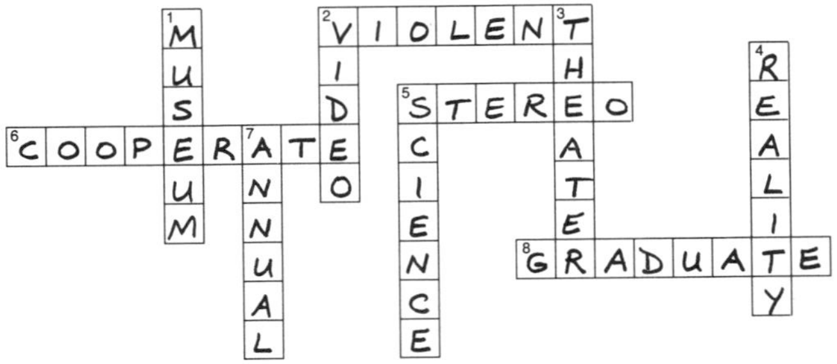

WORKSHEET 38–G

Review the accent patterns below. Copy the words by syllables, writing the accented syllables in the boxes.

The accent is usually on the first syllable in two-syllable words.

stoic	[sto]	ic		fluid	[flu]	id

The accent is usually on the first syllable in three-syllable words.

diagram	[di]	a	gram	nucleus	[nu]	cle	us
linear	[lin]	e	ar	altruism	[al]	tru	ism

The accent is usually on the second syllable in three-syllable words that contain a prefix, root, and suffix.

reaction	re	[ac]	tion	coercion	co	[er]	cion
denial	de	[ni]	al	reliance	re	[li]	ance

The accent is usually on the second syllable in four-syllable words.

geography	ge	[og]	ra	phy
variety	va	[ri]	e	ty
cooperate	co	[op]	er	ate
continuous	con	[tin]	u	ous

WORKSHEET 38–H

Review the accent patterns below. Copy the words by syllables, writing the accented syllables in the boxes.

Accent the syllable just before the ending *-tion*.

creation	cre	[a]	tion		
violation	vi	o	[la]	tion	
coordination	co	or	di	[na]	tion

Accent the syllable just before the ending *-ic*.

stoic	[sto]	ic		
poetic	po	[et]	ic	
bionic	bi	[on]	ic	
altruistic	al	tru	[is]	tic

Accent the syllable just before the ending *-tial*.

influential	in	flu	[en]	tial

Accent the syllable just before the ending *-ity*.

priority	pri	[or]	i	ty	
annuity	an	[nu]	i	ty	
ambiguity	am	bi	[gu]	i	ty

WORKSHEET 38–I

Sometimes it is hard to tell whether a word has a vowel/vowel combination or a double-vowel sound. If you aren't sure, try the double-vowel sound first. If that doesn't result in a recognizable word, pronounce it as a V/V combination.

Example: In *oil*, *oi* says /oi/. In *stoic*, *oi* says /ō-ĭ/.

In these word pairs, one word has a double vowel (VV) and one has a vowel/vowel combination (V/V). Say the words. If the vowels are sounded together as a double vowel, draw an arc (‿) under them. If the vowels are sounded separately, draw a line between them and mark the first vowel long. One pair has been done for you.

true	oasis	priest	* fluent	toe
* cruel	oatmeal	* science	flue	* poetry
reason	Cooper	stoic	ruin	* quiet
* react	* cooperate	spoil	cruise	grief
* cruelty	coagulate	brief	linear	* museum
untrue	coasting	* client	heathen	maneuver

Write the fifteen V/V words below.

cruel	client
react	fluent
cruelty	ruin
oasis	linear
cooperate	poetry
coagulate	quiet
science	museum
stoic	

Have another student test you on spelling the starred words. They are practical spelling words.

My score: __________ words correct.

WORKSHEET 38–J

The words below are commonly used V/V words. Underline the V/V combinations, draw a line between the vowels, and mark the first vowel long. Then write the word under the correct heading.

trial	annual	hideous	variety	coordination
fluent	diary	fluid	cereal	cooperate
poetry	anxiety	science	theater	client
realize	ideal	museum	graduate	truant

ē/V	ī/V	ō/V
realize	trial	poetry
ideal	diary	coordination
hideous	anxiety	cooperate
museum	science	
cereal	variety	
theater	client	

ū/V

fluent
annual
fluid
graduate
truant

Find and circle the twenty words above in the puzzle below. The words can be found in a straight line across or up and down.

T	H	E	A	T	E	R	C	O	O	R	D	I	N	A	T	I	O	N	I	D	E	A	L
R	F	C	E	R	E	A	L	T	Y	C	O	O	P	E	R	A	T	E	A	I	N	N	D
I	L	S	R	E	A	L	I	Z	E	H	I	D	E	O	U	S	M	U	S	E	U	M	I
A	U	N	A	N	X	I	E	T	Y	O	R	I	R	Y	A	P	O	E	T	R	Y	A	A
L	I	E	N	T	A	N	N	U	A	L	S	C	I	E	N	C	E	L	T	Y	U	L	R
I	D	V	A	R	I	E	T	Y	G	R	A	D	U	A	T	E	F	L	U	E	N	T	Y

WORKSHEET 38–K

Your teacher will dictate some practical spelling words. Say the words aloud as you write them under the correct heading.

Remember: If you have trouble with a schwa sound or a schwa ending, try one vowel. If it doesn't look right, try another.

ē/V	ī/V	ō/V
ideal	science	poetry
realize	client	coordinate
museum	variety	going
hideous	trial	cooperate
theater	diary	

ū/V
cruelty
truant
fluid
annual
graduate
fluent

Review: In the words above you divide between the vowels.

In these words the first vowel has its long sound.

Proofing Practice: Three common List 38 words are misspelled in each of the sentences below. Correct them as shown.

1. Two seniors will ~~gradjooate~~ graduate with a major in computer ~~sience~~ science and a minor in ~~jeeography~~ geography.
2. Your ~~cliant~~ client will ~~cooprate~~ cooperate more when his ~~angziety~~ anxiety is better controlled.
3. During the ~~anuel~~ annual board meeting, a ~~voriety~~ variety of entertainment was provided in the ~~muzeum~~ museum.

WORKSHEET 38–L

Sometimes V/V words are formed when a prefix that ends with a vowel is added to a root that begins with a vowel. This happens sometimes with the prefixes *re-*, *pre-*, *de-*, and *co-*.

Circle the prefixes and pronounce the words. Then use twelve of the words to complete the sentences below.

Remember: *pre-* = before; earlier; in front of   *de-* = away; remove; undo
re- = again; repeated; restored   *co-* = jointly; together; mutually

preoccupied	reappraised	deodorant	reappear	reinforce
cooperative	realize	readjustment	coalesce	deactivated
reimbursed	reenter	coordinate	deicer	preoperative
reorganize	coagulate	preignition	coincided	prearrange

1. In Minneapolis winters, people need a deicer to prevent ice from building up on the car's windshield.
2. Before operating on you, a doctor should perform a preoperative physical examination.
3. We used a room deodorant to get rid of the smoky smell.
4. After the war was over, the third regiment was deactivated.
5. The club president reimbursed me for the supplies I had bought.
6. She will reenter the work force after her maternity leave.
7. After we built an addition, the city inspector reappraised our house and said it was worth more money.
8. I wondered if the magician's rabbit would ever reappear.
9. Although the technician had already adjusted the color on my television, I had to request a readjustment because the picture was too red.
10. You seem very preoccupied; are you worried about something?
11. Brian is not willing to work together with the rest of us; he is not a cooperative person.
12. Because their working hours coincided, Stuart and Joel decided to form a car pool.

WORKSHEET 38–M

Complete the puzzle, using the words below. Use a dictionary to look up the meanings of unfamiliar words.

influenza	chaotic	minuet	iodine	triumphant
iota	oasis	coordinate	truant	cruelty
meander	reaction	stoic	annual	altruistic
cameo				riotous

Across

7. A watering hole in the desert
9. Flu; an acute contagious disease with fever and pain
10. Arrange in proper order; put in proper relations; harmonize
12. Victorious; successful
13. Meanness; unkindness
14. Unselfish
15. A substance used to kill germs on cuts and wounds

Down

1. A slow, stately dance
2. To wind around; to wander
3. A precious stone, carved with a raised design
4. A tiny bit; a very small quantity
5. Boisterous; disorderly; in a riot
6. Action in response to some influence
8. Self-controlling; calm in pain or pleasure
10. Confused or disordered; in chaos
11. Yearly
12. Someone who skips school

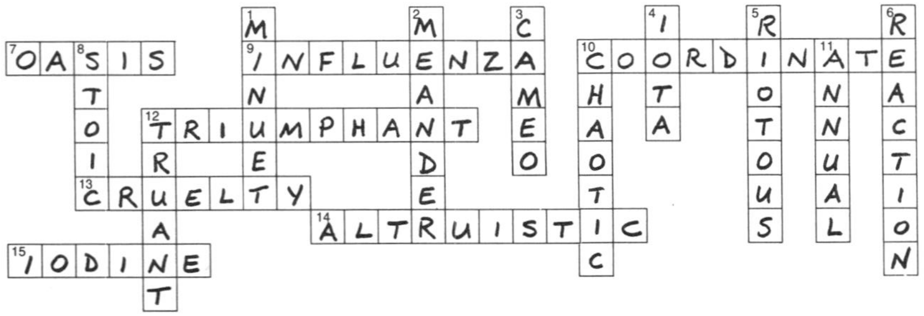

WORKSHEET 38–N

Read the following sentences and circle all the List 38 words that you can find.

1. The pioneer's diary recorded the chaos caused by the influenza epidemic in Iowa.
2. If Ryan violates the terms of his parole, he will have to stand trial.
3. There was a boa constrictor in the zoology wing of the science museum.
4. The audience was quiet when Stuart and Leona began their violin duet.
5. The annual graduation ceremony and class reunions were held in the theater.
6. The scientist and friar held different opinions on the theory of creation.
7. Leon Ryan is a stoic man; he does not seem to react to the cruelty and violence of prison life.
8. I have a variety of rings for sale: cameo, diamond, or gold.
9. Ms. Stuart is fluent in several Siamese dialects.
10. It required cooperation and coordination to run the biannual rodeo in Minneapolis.

Take out a piece of blank paper. Your teacher will dictate three of the sentences above for you to write.

Now select ten words from List 38 and create a short story or a descriptive paragraph that uses those words. Be creative and avoid repetition!

Reading Accuracy: Demonstrate your accuracy in reading and spelling List 38 words. Your teacher will select ten words to read and ten practical spelling words for you to spell. Record your scores on the Accuracy Checklist. Work toward 90–100 percent accuracy.

Reading Proficiency: Now build up your reading fluency with List 38 words. Decide on your rate goal with your teacher. Record your progress on the Proficiency Graph.

My goal for reading List 38 is ________ words per minute with two or fewer errors.

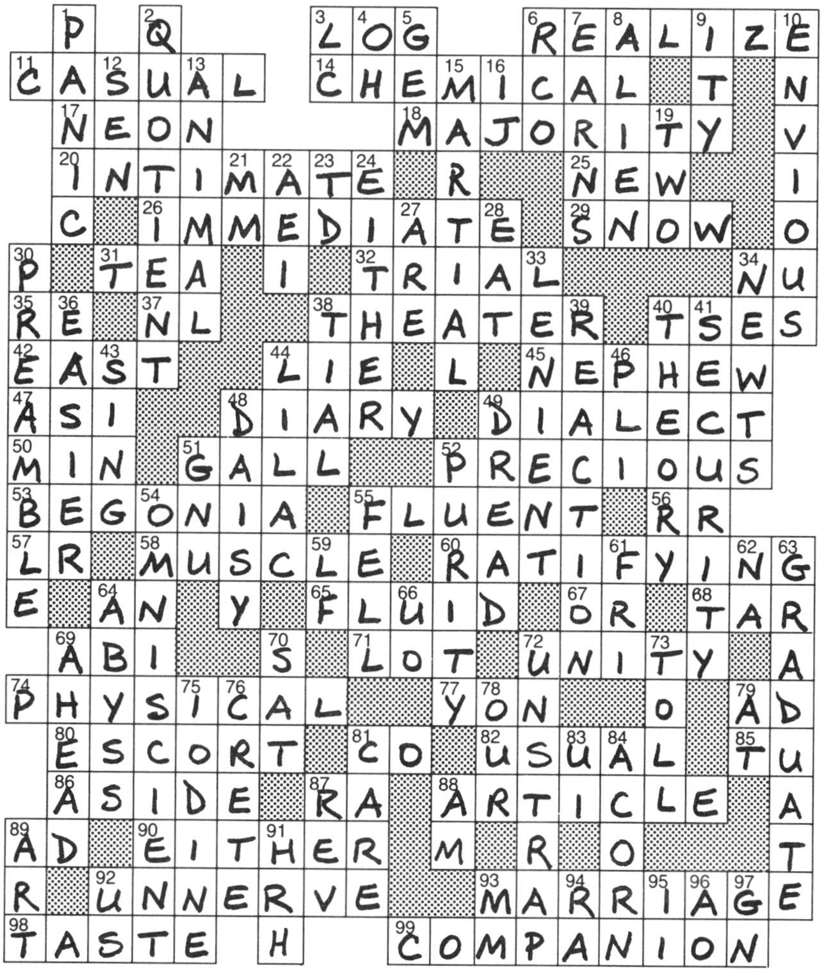

ACCURACY CHECKLIST

Megawords 7, Lists 34–38

Student ______________________________

Record accuracy score as a fraction: # correct / # attempted

List	Examples	Check Test Scores Date:		Reading			Spelling		
		Reading	Spelling						
34. Unaccented *i* = /ə/ or *ĭ*	arbitrate quality political								
35. Unaccented *i* = /ē/ and Unaccented *u*	zodiac continual								
36. Unaccented *i* = /y/	opinion million								
37. *ti* and *ci* Endings	ambitious delicious								
38. Advanced V/V Combinations	creation graduate								
Review: Lists 34–38									

PROFICIENCY GRAPH

Student___________________________

Goal___________________________

•———• Words Read Correctly

×———× Errors

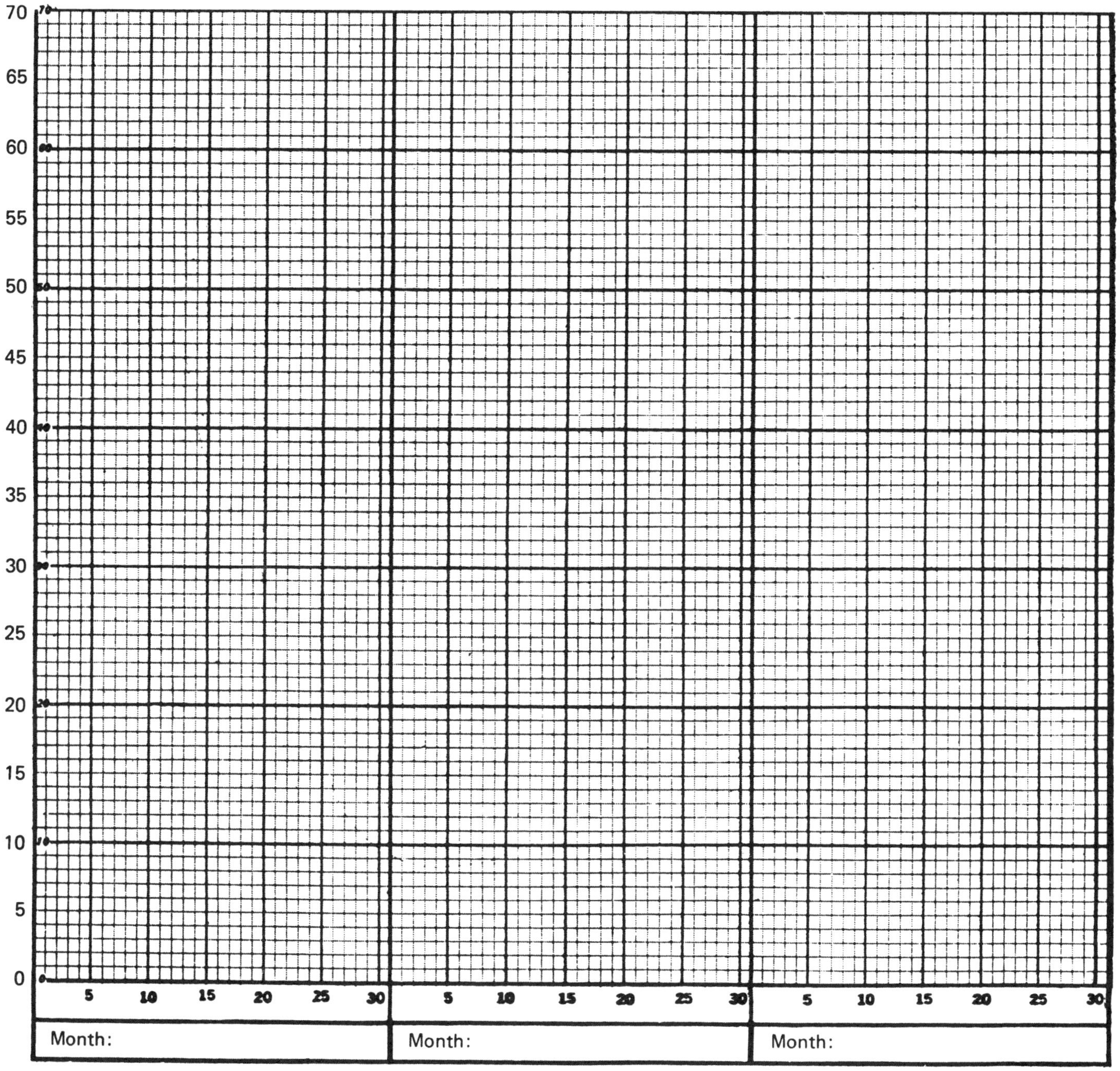

Calendar Days

EXAMINER'S RECORDING FORM—READING

Check Test: Lists 34–38

Megawords 7

Name ______________________ Date ______________________

34. Unaccented *i* = /ə/

optimist
ventilate
humidity
political
captivity

\# correct ________

35. Unaccented *i* = /ē/ and *u*

chariot
actual
document
sodium
malaria

\# correct ________

36. Unaccented *i* = /y/

communion
familiar
gardenia
rebellious
behavior

\# correct ________

37. *ti* and *ci* Endings

sequential
ancient
infectious
artificial
omniscient

\# correct ________

38. Advanced V/V Combinations

anxiety
diary
ambiguity
coordination
reunion

\# correct ________

Total Correct ________
Total Possible ___25___

STUDENT'S READING COPY

Check Test: Lists 34–38

Megawords 7

34.
- optimist
- ventilate
- humidity
- political
- captivity

35.
- chariot
- actual
- document
- sodium
- malaria

36.
- communion
- familiar
- gardenia
- rebellious
- behavior

37.
- sequential
- ancient
- infectious
- artificial
- omniscient

38.
- anxiety
- diary
- ambiguity
- coordination
- reunion

SCOPE AND SEQUENCE CHART

Megawords 1 Six Types of Syllables; Five Syllabication Rules	**List 1** Compound Words	**List 2** VC/CV Closed Syllables	**List 3** VC/CV Closed & Silent-*e* Syllables	**List 4** VC/CV Closed & *r*-Controlled Syllables	**List 5** V/CV	**List 6** VC/V	**List 7** /*Cle*	**List 8** V/V
Megawords 2 Common Prefixes and Suffixes	**List 9** *-ly, -ty, -ful -ment, -fully -ness, -some -less, -s, -es*	**List 10** *-ing, -er -est, -en -ish, -y*	**List 11** Three Sounds of *ed*	**List 12** Spelling Patterns—Vowel Suffixes	**List 13** *re-, de-, ex- pre-, per- sub-, un- in-, pro-*	**List 14** *inter-, a- trans-, con- dis-, mis- ad-, ab-, ob-*		
Megawords 3 Schwa Sound	**List 15** *-al, -ic*	**List 16** *-it, -ite -et, -ate*	**List 17** Middle-Syllable Schwa	**List 18** *-ant, -ance -ent, -ence*	**List 19** *-ive, -ice -ace, -ine -ain*			
Megawords 4 Advanced Suffixes	**List 20** *-er, -or, -ar -ard, -ward*	**List 21** *-tion*	**List 22** *-sion -cian*	**List 23** *-ous -age*	**List 24** *-tu-, -ture -sure*	**List 25** *-able, -ible Cle*		
Megawords 5 Vowel Variations	**List 26** Vowel Combinations with *o*	**List 27** Vowel Combinations with *a*	**List 28** Vowel Combinations with *e*	**List 29** Vowel Sounds of *y*				
Megawords 6 Consonant Variations	**List 30** Sounds of *ch, ph,* and *que*	**List 31** Soft *c*	**List 32** Soft *g*	**List 33** V*r*V and V*rr*V Combinations				
Megawords 7 Unaccented Vowels and Advanced V/V	**List 34** *-i-, -ity -ical i* = /ə/	**List 35** *i* = /ē/ *u* = /ə/ or /ū/	**List 36** *i* = /y/	**List 37** *ti* & *ci* = /sh/	**List 38** Advanced V/V			
Megawords 8 Assimilated Prefixes	**List 39** *com-*	**List 40** *ad-*	**List 41** *sub-*	**List 42** *ob-, dis-*	**List 43** *ex-, syn-*	**List 44** *in-*		

EPS®
EDUCATORS PUBLISHING SERVICE
800.225.5750
www.epsbooks.com

ISBN 0-8388-1837-4
9 780838 818374